Table of Contents

The Human Race by Madhavendra Puri

In times before the Human Race
There was peace by Krishna's Grace.
Then God created the heavenly man
And then his woman to embrace
And populate the Human Race

A goal was set then for this race
To pass beyond the edge of space.
This prize was good and oh so fine
Enticing all of human kind
To set their eyes upon God's face
And live eternal in His grace

That alone was best of all
In fact I'd say it was a ball
To be behind this Heavenly Wall
And palace hall of stones and chain
The golden type that should remain
Beneath the ground from whence it came
For simple monetary gain

The race for this became insane
For men who saw the golden chain
And knew the power of the brain
Could multiply our race again
And conquer all in their domain
The conquest was the human brain

To manipulate the Human Race
Or those who sought to see God's face
By sounds supplied at speeds of light
Through waves that travel in the night
Reflecting off their main delight
The golden laden caves at night.

In the emptiness that lies beyond
That flash within this space at night
Phosphates of iron and meteorite
Another conquest to be found
Far above this Heavenly Ground
Sometimes admitting quite a sound
Reverberating to the ground
Spinning everything around
Upon the road of Heaven bound

The guys and gals they're all around
Rocking to the fateful sound
Bouncing off the Holy Ground
Rock and Roll it was the sound
That set us off and Heaven Bound

According to this very sound
Reverberating to the ground
Bouncing all of us around
And rocking on the Holy Ground
Me myself and I were there
We're letting down our strands of hair
We're here and there and everywhere

In between the sights and sounds
Reverberating to the ground
Creating such an awesome sound
And rocking all of us around
While we wold dance on Holy Ground

Myself and I looked straight at me
The three of us a multiplicity
A simple seaman said to me
However can that ever be
A Multiplicity-of me

Some would call this reality
That is Me, Myself and I
I bet he has an alibi
And probably he is a spy
Me Myself and I

Madhavendra Puri   **Colonel Oliver W. Pepper IV**   **George Harrison Haltom III**

The incredible Adventures of the Aristocratic Pauper

Memories meander through time on a voyage over oceans and ages. One of them traveled back to the day God said, "Let us make man in our image, and after our own likeness". Remembering these words came easy, because at that time we were talking about how the Neanderthals were still dragging their knuckles. Mother Nature's course of evolution had done a fine job so far, but God knew He could do it better.

God made man in His own image, both male and female; He created them and blessed them. God gave them dominion over every living thing that moved upon the earth, including the cattle of the land, even the fish of the seas, and the fowls of the air. Every living thing that moved on the earth was a gift to humanity. whose purpose was to subdue and replenish the earth. God said to be fruitful and multiply, this is His Divine Will.

When God created man there were living beings throughout the universe, and even upon a planet that evolved naturally. The original beings were 144,000 angels assigned to watch over and serve God's creation. We watched in awe as the beginning of time became manifest before our very eyes. We watched this all week long! Of course in God's Kingdom time is not measured in earth's twenty-four hour days. There are millions of earth years in just one of God's days, and seven days in God's house is really quite a long time compared to a week on this little planet.

The book you now have in your hand could take into account the 5,000 years that we spent just writing literature, poems, letters, translations, commentaries. and our thoughts for your edification; many I recall, and others that I recognize as being my own or messages God has sent me to deliver. The Autobiography of an Angel begins in 1965, but could have ended in the summer of '67 if God had not intervened on that sixth of May when the police attacked me with prejudice and vengeance! Instead of dropping dead like an ordinary man, a journey across the USA is in order.

With only my classical guitar, a well-practiced thumb, and more faith than imaginable, I set out for a distant shore. This is a true story about the revelations that enlightened me, and set many free. The self-realization that follows when a person is free from the bondage that is the fear of death is so enlightening it is equal to being born again. The Lord said that you must be born again meaning at the very least a spiritual rebirth.

One day while walking along the road to our house and looking toward a mountain range beyond the lake, inspiration hit unexpectedly. It was In a very straight forward manner, my prayer to God the Father made its way to heaven. Love for God was only natural and made me want to be like Jesus in every way; to walk anywhere necessary in order to render my service with such devotion that people would recognize the similitude. With just a desire for the freedom from the concerns about food, clothes, and shelter in order to be God's servant, I set out on a journey through this life that should be a stroll in the garden.

The first journey led to the Box Canyon Monastery known as the Fountain of the World. This was the Order of Melchizedek, or the similitude of it. The brothers of this order never cut their hair, instead they kept it in braids. The robes they had were gray with a silver sash they tied. Roman sandals and trimmed beards made the look more saintly and appealing. A creek flowed near the compound and buildings made of rock and mortar stood a midst the tall oak trees. They designed the meeting hall around a large oak tree with branches extending beyond the roof. A stage was built front and center where the group met.

While sitting beside the stream a melody came into my mind that expressed the serenity of the moment. Adlibitum seemed right for the title, I did not understand the meaning of the word I wrote it on the top of the manuscript any way. Later that day someone told me this is the Latin term for at liberty. It was early morning and the sun was about to rise. After climbing to the peak of the mountain to watch the sun come into sight, I realized that the earth was turning as it came in to view. Suddenly a big golden robed figure appeared from within the rays of the sun, moving closer and closer with His arms reaching out in a peaceful gesture. This was a manifestation of God! As He drew near I closed my eyes because I did feel unworthy to look directly into the face of our Heavenly Father. A sudden gust of wind rushed by and words rang loud and clear, "You are doing a fine job my boy, keep up the good work."

God had just spoken, and this is undeniable. He so real that my vow to serve Him in a manner that would keep Him pleased motivated me to offering my body as a temple. He took me up on this and lives there still. Yet in the midst this experience, God's sense of humor became evident with what may have been one heck of an angelic joke.

The mountain's rocky surface was uncomfortable to sit on; so, it seemed to be a good idea to take off my jeans and fold them into a cushion. Being half naked on a mountaintop watching God come out of the eastern sky is a memorable event for sure, but what happened next seems more like a miracle. That gust of wind must have blown away my Levis, or they just disappeared. It would not be wise to hitchhike in that condition, and even more foolish to try to walk all the way. Then out of nowhere a pickup truck came driving along the fire trail. The driver said this was his annual inspection of Box Canyon to make sure the path was clear in case of a wild fire. He offered a ride and pretended not to notice his passenger was a half-naked hippie with an unusual glow.

Elder Asaiah, head priest of the Fountain of the World. was my spiritual guide. He was a friend from many lives. He was a devotee of Krishna, who accepted Melchizedek as Spiritual Master. Melchizedek chose the High Priest of the Order, and that selection was me, the one whom they awaited. Brother Johokum was a member who looked like Jesus in the flesh. He was cool as a beatnik from the fifties, and mystical as any true saint. He gave me a golden robe that was made in India for the chosen one. It happened one Saturday evening during the weekly talent show; he said he had been waiting sixty-nine mental years to present this robe.

Krishna Venta built the Fountain of the World during the mid forties. He was the same Melchizedek mentioned in Genesis, and in Hebrews 7 of the Bible. He is a priest that abides forever; without descent according to scripture, neither mother nor father, but made like Christ. This was an unusual man, so astounding that Abram gave a tenth of the spoils from the slaughter of Sodom and Gomorrah. Abram himself would become the father of a great nation of Chosen People according to Melchizedek, the King of Salem, also called King of Righteousness, and King of Peace. The word Jeru translates into new, and Abram's people would occupy New Salem, or Jerusalem. Melchizedek is the link between the Hindu, Jewish and Christian faiths. We all serve the same Lord, and Master. He is the Living God and is with us continually.

The next journey on this path to enlightenment was to Escondido Canyon Retreat in Latigo Canyon, just north of Malibu overlooking the Pacific Coast. A green three-story Christmas tree house built near the top of the mountain became home, and the retreat was the church where a congregation soon formed. The tree house was in the center of a Christmas tree lot. We sold trees to transplant after the holidays. There was a large garden with fruit trees, vegetables, and herbs in raised beds that were terraced along the hills contour. This was our Garden of Eden. We had herbs growing in the garden and though out the Escondido Canyon Retreat. The Spring of Eternal Life broke through the rocks and down a waterfall into a creek that flowed into a pool. A pump would return the water to the spring and it flowed constantly. The retreat had a beautiful lawn of imported grass, and ferns from tropical climates, a wide variety of flowers and vegetables, and fungi feeding fig trees. The sprinkler system watered everything, all the way to the Cathedral of the Oaks, where our services respected all religions mentioned.

Mr. McCoy owned the property, and was an interesting fellow. He was extremely well off. Two gardeners lived in a cabin near the tree house, and worked there on the property full time. Some days we would run to the beach and gather seaweed for Mr. McCoy. He would grind it in a blender with fresh herbs and spices to put on our salads. It looked like guacamole and tasted like ordinary green goop. It would have been great to live there forever, but fate would not allow it In fact, it would not be too long before this adventure went from heaven on earth to hell itself.

I walked and hitchhiked between the Fountain of the World in Box Canyon, and the Escondido Canyon Retreat, always carrying my guitar to write songs about current events like a minstrel, or my songs of praise just like a prophet. Topanga Canyon was on this route and a hippie haven where a multitude of acid heads and Rock & Roll musicians dwelt. Before long most of them became friends and fans from playing for dinner at the Moon Fire Inn or the Thespian Restaurant. The Coral was the main watering hole and some very popular bands like Spirit, ELO, even Jimmy Hendrix would play his latest hits to a crowd of rocking sixty's hippies.

Jay Ferguson was the lead singer with the band Spirit, and a friend since Junior High. Sometimes he would take a break and I would set in. When the strobe lights started flashing and the band began rocking, it was like being in another dimension in space and time. Love beads were in fashion, and everyone wore the strangest outfits. They were all non-conformists at heart, but in reality more like a representation of a generation gone to pot. The pungent aroma of cannabis filled the air, and the vibration of pure love saturated the atmosphere while a hundred bodies swayed to the beat of the different drummer. The sound of Rock and Roll playing into the night echoed through the canyon walls. Love was in the air, and I was there to enjoy it.

Late in the spring in '66, there was a man claiming to be Michael the Archangel. He played a Martin guitar and was as free as a bird. We met at Pierce Jr. College and formed a mystical bond only two angels could understand. We became a duo called "Just Us" and booked a concert at the Theatrical Center in the college. He had a cabin in Topanga Canyon, and it was there he served Korean Ginseng Root and Bancha Tea, an hallucinatory tea grown in China. It was the mixture of the energy from the ginseng root, and the effects of the Bancha Tea that was equal to any LSD trip available on the market. The good thing is that these were legal and easy to purchase from a health food store, or herbalist.

Later that night after leaving the cabin and walking through a moon lit forest, the smell of the wild flowers and trees seemed enchanting. Wandering down the hill beside a creek, the trees seemed to come alive and speak clearly. Nature was inspiring and timeless, so I took off my watch and hung it on a branch. Never again to be a slave to time, watching the clock or worrying about what time it is.

That night brought clarity and understanding of what the Bible meant in the Book of Revelations, That an angel with the little book and loud voice would someday speak to the entire world declaring that time should be no more. This was my destiny, and what had to be done. I needed to write the little book and tell the world what would happen in the last days. The Falling Figs Journal should take three and a half years to complete, or so I thought; but it has taken over forty-seven, and we still have a few years before it's finished, but here it is, the little book !!! Go ahead take this book and eat it, or read it. When you digest it, you will understand what it means to be sweet as honey in your mouth, but in your belly it will be so bitter.

On my twentieth birthday a few friends dropped by to celebrate. One of them sang in a band called Styx. He gave me some M&Ms as a present, and told me to chew up a certain red one. I never tried LSD before, and I was unaware the M&Ms were spiked with acid. Nevertheless, that night my life would change forever. We piled into a VW bug and went to a jam session with a group of musicians in Woodland Hills, We partied like rock stars. Why not! We really were rock stars, and this was our time to shine.

On our way back the cops stopped us for a burnt out taillight. We all got out as ordered. and I said, "Hi Brother" to the officer. He said that I was not his brother. I told him that according to my religion all men were brothers. He then told me to put my hands on top of my head because he was going to frisk me for weapons. All I had on was a pair of cut off shorts and sandals. What was there to frisk? He immediately grabbed my balls and squeezed them. I turned to face him and tell that no man had ever touched me there, and to watch where he put his hands. He then began administering a choke hold and squeezed my neck so hard that the blood to my brain stopped. I felt the electrifying sting of death in my body, and it felt as if my soul departed.

Suddenly I surprised everyone by passing right through his forearm and standing up. I turned to him and said that he was a fool for doing that, because he could not hurt me. The jerk was not amused, and he and his partner attacked me a second time. They threw me to the ground and slammed my head into the asphalt. One cop handcuffed me while the other stomped on my face with his boots and ground my head into the asphalt parking lot. After they had me in cuffs, one of them pulled a little package out of his pocket and sprinkled a couple of marijuana seeds into his palm. Then he jammed his hand into my pocket and pulled it out as if he had just discovered my stash. What a joke! Four tenths of a micro gram of debris, and he was going to try to send me to prison for twenty years.

They threw me in the back of the squad car and told me to shut up. He asked if I had ever seen sausage, then told me if he heard one more word out of me that I would be his breakfast. I suppose that meant I had the right to remain silent. I looked directly at him and thought. "Go to hell you asshole". I knew that such a curse would be his fate, and I was in no mood to show mercy. They had no way of knowing that I had been accepted by the Los Angeles Police to enter the academy and become an officer, but was under weight.

They took me to the hospital to patch up my wounds. Then hauled me off to jail. It was ten days before my family would bail me out, and only on the condition that I check into Camarillo Mental Hospital. It was my only alternative; plead not guilty because of insanity, or lose freedom for about twenty years.

The Beatles song Come Together spoke to me in a very personal manner. John Lennon is a true prophet, and the reincarnation of Saint John the Divine. I could feel the love they shared with the world in every note they played. They hooked up with a guru who taught them the path of Transcendental Meditation. That worried me because I was not sure if Maharishi was a positive spiritual force, or a negative entity leading them astray. Looks can be deceiving, and Maharishi had the look of an angel on a mission. Was that mission to save the souls of who ever came to him for spiritual guidance, or trap therm and claim their souls with his non-sense.

One Saturday night at the Fountain of the World, I gave a sermon on the fulfillment of the ninth chapter of Revelations that describes the Beatles. Soon Charles Manson was telling his family that The Beatles were the locusts with faces like men and hair like women, and that he was king of the locusts. Confusion was everywhere. I had to figure out where all the pieces fit in this puzzle. Like who was with God, and who were the false prophets. I sure wouldn't want to be among them, and loose my soul for all eternity. I would never change my priesthood and serve a lesser God. I could recognize the warning signs, and this trip to the mental institution was an attempt by the state to control my mind, while they brainwash me into conformity with society. Well that would never happen in my lifetime Not in the land of the free and the home of the brave.

I checked in to the hospital voluntarily, ready to play their game and outwit them in the process. They had a preconceived notion that I was paranoid schizophrenic with delusions of grandeur. Thanks to Dr. Irving Matzner, a friend of my mother. He wrote a letter to the court saying he had diagnosed me as having this condition. That aggravated me because I never spoke to him. He just took her word for it and wrote the letter as if I had actually been to his office. This lie has caused more harm to my life than all of the eccentricities I exhibit could ever cause. The repercussions were devastating at that time, and still are today. It follows me around like a ball and chain.

I was married during the time this all happened. My wife was pregnant with our second child but she refused to join me in my quest for truth. She chose to take the easy way out and used Dr. Matzner's letter as the grounds for divorce. After she brought the court papers to the hospital I never saw her again. This is all the mention she deserves.

Before I decided to leave the mental institution, I had an unusual experience. It has lingered in my sub conscious, and I can still picture it. There was a young patient called Julius Christopolos. He was a small homosexual who thought he was Jesus. I was near the nurse's station when he walked up to me and planted a big wet kiss right on my lips. I could see why he was here, the dude was whack-o. The attendants saw this and took immediate action. They came after us with hypodermic needles filled with Thorazine, and overdosed us out of spite. I barely made it to my bed in time to pass out. The effect I was experiencing was like my mind shutting down. I looked at the walls and they began to melt away. The ceiling started to melt then disappeared before I started floating towards the clouds. I looked down and saw myself sleeping soundly. or just laying very still.

Apparently the attendants had just killed me and I was going to heaven. Then out of nowhere a cool dude dressed in a white robe led me to a serene mountain side with a beautiful stream flowing next to a small log cabin. He then opened the door and showed me what was to be my reward. Someday this would be my own place, but not yet. He told me to go back and finish what I had set out to do. This was my guardian angel. He knew everything that I ever did and let me know that I had nothing to be ashamed of. He pointed to the direction I came from, and the next thing I remember was waking up from very deep sleep.

I decided I had enough of this place and left Camarillo the next day without even saying goodbye. On the way back to my old stomping grounds I found a Renaissance Fair in progress. There were hundreds of people dressed in medieval costumes walking around enjoying all the sights. Booths portraying various activities common in the 16th Century like the blacksmiths and mid wives were set up on these fairgrounds. I had escaped from a mental institution and here I was in a time and place that seemed to be at least 400 years from where I came from when I began my journey.

Exhilarating best describes my mood, the Topanga Minstrel was back! and In a very good place where I could captivate a live audience. They were there to be entertained, and I was sure eager to please. This was a generous crowd too. The tips helped me get home. It is somewhat ironic however. I was in one place where a bunch of people thought they were someone else who was from the past, and they were locked up. Then I wound up in a place where everyone acted as if they were someone else, mostly from the past, and these people were being paid for it!

I began to write songs in a book I called the Falling Figs Journal. The title is a biblical connotation hinting that when the fig tree is ripe Jesus would return. I would type up the pages and take them to the copy center to publish a limited edition. Then I would sell them to my friends and who ever wanted a collector's edition of fine literature. Falling Figs Music Publishing Company was born as I started recording songs and selling cassettes tapes along with the journal. I would use different pen names for the characters I portrayed in the writing styles. Oliver Wimbleton Pepper became my songwriting pseudonym, and Father Orville O. McKenzie wrote the sermons that no one would hear. Oliver Pepper's main influence came from Oliver Wendell Holmes, Henry Wadsworth Longfellow, and Sargent Pepper's Lonely Hearts Club Band. Father Mackenzie wrote like Ralph Waldo Emerson; deeply philosophical, and spiritually enlightened. The fool on the hill was alive and well, but nobody knew his name, or cared to know him because they thought he was insane.

In November of 1967, I ran into an old friend from high school who asked if I wanted to be ordained. He told me that he could do it right there on the spot. I accepted and became an ordained minister with the First Church of God the Father. This non-sectarian church accepted every religion as a path to God the Father. I already believed that, and was glad there was someone else that saw things in the same light. I started visiting the founder of the church, Bishop Brimm, in his North Hollywood office. We talked about reincarnation, the eastern religions like Hindus, the yoga's and followers of Buddhism. The Christian churches I grew up in all taught that these were false religions. I worried about those people and needed to know how they all were linked to the same God. The Bishop did not have a solution, but he did have faith. He believed we were all saints and asked me to remember him as Saint Claude when I called my church to come together.

The marijuana trial date finally came around in the May of 1968. The judge looked and me and then looked at the two cops, he threw out the assault charge right off the bat. He said he could not believe that a little guy my size would ever assault two police officers, and told the prosecutors that he believed the charges were an exaggeration. Then he looked at the minute amount of cannabis they offered as evidence and proclaimed it an unusable amount. He dismissed the drug possession charge too. It was apparent I had committed no crime, but then he read the letter Dr. Matzner wrote and ordered me to go to another hearing to determine the state of my sanity.

A few weeks later I appeared for this final hearing and was surprised by the outcome. I went into a room where a psychiatrist asked me a couple of questions, I answered them and he said thank you and left. Then I went into the hearing and they asked me if I was Jesus. I told them, "No I am not". I remembered the prayer when I asked God to let me be so much like Jesus that people would think I was Him. The psychiatrist snapped back rhetorically, "Then who are you?", I said, "I am Buddha." The translation of that statement is that I am the enlightened one. This does not mean I actually was the Prince of India who renounced his right to the throne and abandoned his family to become a beggar monk several thousand years ago. I did not say that I was the one who sat under a fig tree to became enlightened when a ripe fig fell into my hands showing me that God would supply my every need. I left that to their imagination.

The judge slammed down the gavel and sentenced to an indefinite stay at Atascadero State Prison for the Criminally Insane. This seemed rather harsh and my dad stood up and told the judge that the church and garden actually existed. I took him there once and he was very impressed. Then to my delight Bishop Brimm placed a call to the judge and spoke on my behalf. The judge listened to the Bishop and recanted his decision. He said thought he would send me to Metropolitan State Hospital for a clinical observation instead.

Shortly after the hearing they took me in shackles and chains to the State Hospital. The cop who brought me there removed the chains after they put me in a locked ward they thought was secure. While he was signing some papers, I noticed a familiar face walking through a corridor behind the room. I walked towards him and followed him out an open door that led to the hos[ital grounds and to the main highway. So I decided to go home and get a few things I needed to make my stay here more enjoyable. I never got a good look at the guy who showed me the way out; he just walked out and disappeared around the corner. I decided to use my guitar case as my luggage, and stashed my guitar in the bushes behind the locked ward I just slipped out of.

I walked across the street and as soon as I put my thumb out a psychedelic painted bus rolled to a stop and opened the door. The old hippie driving that bus didn't have a lot to say. He put some tunes on and handed me a joint. He was on his way to San Francisco and drove me to the Pacific Coast Highway and Topanga Canyon. This was a perfect start to get home. I was on the same street that led to my parent's house. I had less than thirty miles to go, so I got off the bus and walked to where I always hitchhiked through the canyon. A middle-aged guy that looked like a businessman, drove the first car that came around the corner. I never expected him to stop but he did. He even said that he was not accustomed to picking up strangers, but something told him that I would be good company through the canyon, so he picked me up.

He was on his way to Simi Valley and dropped me off right at my parents driveway, on top of the hill in Canoga Park. When I went into the house I found it was empty. I beat my mom and dad home from the court. So I went upstairs and began packing my case with all the things I wanted to have with me like my robe and writings, and some nice things to wear. I could hear the door open and my mom was saying how glad she was that the trial was over. I went downstairs and said "Howdy Folks". My mom passed out on the spot. and my dad wanted to know how I managed to escape. I told him that it was very easy. I just walked out the back door, made my way to the street and stuck my thumb up. The same way I got anywhere I needed to be.

When my mom woke up she called the state hospital to tell them I was home. When she told them how I got away they said I must be crazy because there is no back door to that room. It dawned on me then, I knew who that familiar face was: He is same guy that showed me the cabin in the woods when they overdosed me in Camarillo. My guardian Angel was on the job and it felt good, real good. I went back the next day and sure enough there was neither a back door nor a small corridor in that room. They started giving me a variety of drugs that made me drowsy and caused me to sleep a lot. I could barely talk and had a hard time seeing. The doctor said these side effects would wear off in a short time. I did not want to wait so every time they passed out the medication I would swallow it in front of them like I had to, then walk back to my room and stick my finger down my throat. I put those drugs where they belonged, in the sewer. After a few drug free weeks the staff thought they had cured me and said they would sign the release on one condition. I had to cut my hair and shave my beard so that I would look like a normal member of society. I hated to do it but I did.

John Lennon's new song about Instant Karma was on the air when I left the state hospital. It had a haunting melody and seemed to be referring to what I was going through these past few months. I hoped to meet him some day, and may already have actually. There was a guy in the hospital that said he was John Lennon, but I took that with a grain of salt. He looked something like him, but his hair was short, and he was a little bit plump. He played and sang beautifully, and we spent several days there in the laundry room making music. Nobody bothered us and we picked and grinned for hours on end. Sometimes I wonder if he really was John Lennon, and I just missed an opportunity to get know him. This fellow was only there for a few days, and I never saw him except in the laundry room. We were allowed to have cigarettes, as long as they arrived in a fresh sealed pack. My dad brought me a few packs, and he slipped me a joint of his home grown "Canoga Gold Cannabis".

I guess the instant karma affected my mom in a real way. They lost their hilltop home when the economy took a turn for the worse. It was after my release and we packed up to move to Del Rio, Texas. My dad and I started a small boat company on my Uncle's ranch. We were going to build a hydroplane, and make a mold for reproducing them in fiberglass. We called the boat Miss Adrenaline and named our shop The Canoga Boat Company. It was a hard struggle from the start, and we never were able to attract an investor to help mass produce the little race boats.

I got involved with the Southern Baptist Church in town and kept quiet about my past. Some of my friends and I were able to open a coffeehouse that the church sponsored. We called it the One Way Coffeehouse. We built a stage and opened the door every evening so the local kids to would have a place to hang out play music and just stay out of trouble. Pastor Fred asked me if I would write a song describing the whole salvation experience. It sounded like a good challenge. So I began work on a piece I called The Omniscient Blossom. It turned out beautiful, and I wrote piano and choir parts with a little help from a local piano teacher. The work was so remarkable that both Hardin Simmons and Baylor Universities offered me full scholarships so I could get a degree and become a youth minister. I was already the High Priest and didn't think it was a very good idea. I just wanted to make music and spread a little love and peace around the world.

I met a beautiful singer named Nancy when we competed in a talent contest the city sponsored. Nancy took first place with her rendition of Mr. BO-Jangles. I came in second with a guitar solo. The natural thing to do would be to get together and start making music. We did and soon performed live every Sunday night on the local radio station. As our popularity grew we got the attention of Happy Shahann from Brackettville Texas. He owned Alamo Village, a movie site where they built a replica of the Alamo for a movie starring John Wayne. They also built a town that was supposed to be like San Antonio in the early 1800's. Happy offered me a job to act like the town sheriff, and be a gunslinger. We put on shows daily for the tourist that came to visit. Neil Cole was the other cowboy on the set. It was mandatory on this job to have long shaggy hair and a beard if possible, and If we wanted to smoke a cigarette we had to roll it our self.

The replica of the Alamo was built there for the film The Alamo, with a bunch of great stars. Here I was living a fantasy life pretending to be a cowboy in the 1800's. I wrote several songs while there and improved my style while working with some of the artists that would visit the set. Things seemed to be getting better and going the way I hoped they would before leaving California. The pain was still there, and I resented the way California treated me. I lost everything that was dear to me in one cruel blow. The retreat, the monastery, my wife and kids, in fact everything I worked for had vanished in the gloom. I turned these raw emotions into music and poured out my soul with every song.

Ringo Star had a new song on the air. It was coming over the country stations. He said If you want to sing the blues you would have to pay your dues and you know it don't come easy. Again I felt like the Beatles were kindred spirits and wondered if they knew I was out here trying to work my way back to them on this long and winding road. I was half way across the country and felt I had to move on if I was ever going to reach them. Well the Lord works in mysterious ways, and put me closer suddenly by a turn of events I could not have dreamed up. It started out like any payday at Alamo Village. All the gunslingers would drive to Del Rio and pick up provisions, and spend a few bucks on the way back home.

This time as we drove towards the city I noticed some clouds rolling in on the horizon. When we got to the supermarket in Del Rio, I started to dance around the truck like an Indian. I circled the truck three times just whipping up a storm. A local policeman came over and asked me what I was doing. I told him that I was doing a rain dance. He looked at me funny as I left and went into the store. By the time we finished shopping I could hear the thunder cracking overhead. I went outside and saw huge hailstones breaking windows all around. The cop was still there, he looked at me and said, "I think you over did it Haltom," I just shrugged my shoulders and smiled as we loaded up the car. Our next stop was across the border for some fun i8n Mexico. The food is great, and the beer was as cheap as possible. After putting on a drunken glow, we went back to Texas, a little bit poorer, and none the wiser.

On the way back, the driver spotted a young deer by the roadside. My companions decided to shoot the little guy and take him home to stock up the freezer. I objected, but to no avail. They turned the high beams on and positioned the car so the light would shine in his eyes. The dear just froze, and did not move a muscle. I was surprised how easy it was for them to walk right up and shoot him in the head. There was no sport to it at all, and it was way out of season for hunting.

Well fate took the upper hand and before they could start the car the sheriff was there with his red lights flashing. We made the Texas State Network News that night. The story headline was that the three Alamo Village Gunslingers were in a shootout with a young buck. The news story related the fact that the dear may have died, but the three gunslingers were the real losers. They were right. When we got out of jail and returned to Alamo Village Happy Shahann was not so happy any more, We got our walking papers, packed up our stuff, and headed east to Orlando, Florida.

Neal Cole, the Alamo Village Marshal, let us in on a little secret when we made it to Florida. He had escaped from prison near Tampa less than a year ago. He wanted to visit his girlfriend just to hit he up for some money. We stopped in Daytona Beach Florida for breakfast and gas when he let us in on that little bit of information. I looked around and saw a room for rent sign on a house near where we were and told those guys to wait for me for a couple of minutes. I went to ask the owner how much a poor boy like me would have to pay to live there. We worked out a deal for $3.00 a day.

That was a reasonable price for a room with a private bath, even in those times. I told him I was a priest and wanted to start a church on the beach. I also let him know that I was a good musician and would find work right away. He was a very cool old man and gave me a break. I went back to guys and told them I would be staying here and they could move on without me. They were a little bit surprised, but soon left for parts unknown. I never saw them again, and thought thank God and Greyhound they're gone. I'd hate to be with them if they ever get stopped along the way. Could be a nasty scene, and them cops get mean, and the shoot out isn't in the scene. Shit happens sometime.

My room was in a very nice old rock and mortar style home. It was a two story house with nice trees that had been there for many years. The place looked like it could withstand any hurricane, and probably survived a few already. I unpacked and went out looking for work. I put on my old Levi jeans and a T-shirt. I was ready for anything, I found a guy working on an old steam ship, and went up to him and asked if I could be of any help. I mentioned my last job was at Canoga Boats, and I was an expert at fixing them up. He said get to work and shut up!

I started painting the detail work while he was sanding the deck. He paid me well, and became a friend while I was there. After work I went to the beach and looked around and noticed they let cars drive on the shoreline. There was a neat amphitheater next to the boardwalk where I found a night club called Heavy's. It was the underground hangout for locals, and the Allman Brothers Band played there before Dwayne died, and they moved to Macon, Georgia. The new band was a southern rock group growing in popularity, so I went in and met the owner. After playing a couple of tunes, he hired me to play during the breaks when the rock band took five. I went on at least twice a night from then on, and it was a good career move for me. Heavy's was the top nightclub in Daytona.

A few days after landing in Daytona Beach a news reporter caught wind of me and came to do an interview. They took a picture of me on the beach with my guitar in hand. The reporter wrote a beautiful article telling of my plans to have services at dawn on Sunday mornings. "Sunrise on the Beach Will Be His Service" was the banner headline. The article revealed the fact that I had been ordained, and told of my musical talents. It was nice to walk the streets recognized as a man of the cloth, People introduced themselves to me and treated me kindly. It brought to mind the fact that I seldom told people I was an ordained priest because I didn't want them putting on airs.

Sometimes people would invite me to Sunday dinner so they could pretend to be righteous. Such hypocrisy is commonplace. It was and still is my philosophy that when I meet someone it is a human encounter, with a spiritual undertone that liberates. As I walk the streets I come into contact with a variety of people. Each one with a particular set of circumstances. A derelict on skid row shows the wear and tear not only from the extremities of his tattered clothes, but in a certain pleading that emanates from within his eyes. The wrinkles speak for themselves; life is hard for some. I see it every day, and it is the division of mankind through judgment. An arrogant fundamentalist shuns the homeless vagabond, and wears prosperity like status symbol. They surround themselves with every creature comfort money can buy, and look at the vagabond with disdain. While from a universal concept there is a different picture. The homeless vagabond is actually an angel inheriting it all. These material things possess the rich man, but In the end we come to the same toll bridge and have to pay the price. The rich man cannot take any of it with him, and the angel remains with dominion over it all. It's quite a turnabout and is fair play.

The days in Daytona Beach with endless peaceful walks by the ocean, drifted into long nights at Heavy's. A midst the blare of rock and roll, the smoke in the air reflected the black light's glare and appeared like a foggy haze so thick you could cut it with a knife. The rock and roll musicians would whip the crowd into frenzy, and bodies would sway to the rhythm, while strobe lights break these images into glimpses of life between darkness and light. I knew my mission. I was there to perform. When the singer would say, "We'll be right back after a break". He would introduce me to a crowd that needed some rest. With just a classical guitar and a voice like Bob Dylan's, I would soothe them with melodies and the ideas I put into rhyme and rhythm. They were a minstrel's message of current events that included my discontent with the war in Vietnam, and the political ideology that Marijuana Possession was punishable with long prison sentences.

The political climate of our generation was hot and heavy with memories of better times. "A Day in the Life" was my favorite Beatles song. My version would always get the attention, while the song by Bob Dylan called "Don't Think Twice" would bring my former wife to mind. By the time I got the crowd settled down the rockers would be ready to whip them back into frenzy. It was manic and it was real at the same time.

Not far down the road from Daytona Beach, in a little town called Winter Haven, was a coffeehouse with an attentive crowd that appreciated my music. I would hitchhike the fifty miles just to share a night of love with these kids. One night I believe Cat Stevens was on stage doing a concert. He was electrifying and a tough act to follow. He told us he had just released a new song he called "Peace Train" along with "Morning Has Broken". A song he learned from the Baptist Church Hymnal. It sent chills down my spine. Stevens converted soon after that to the Islamic Faith, and hung up his guitar. I'm glad for two reasons; one is I believe that if you serve God in any religion you won't go wrong, and second the man is stiff competition in the music business. The Bible is right when it stated all things work for the good for those who love the Lord.

Bud Richards will always remain my fondest memory of Daytona Beach. He owned a small restaurant and I was welcome to come sing a song or two for the morning crowd. This kept me well fed, and ready for the day's journey. Bud informally adopted me because I reminded him of his son Dr. R. C. Richards III PhD. He had just graduated from the University of Colorado in Denver, and Bud told me if I ever got in trouble with the law just to say that I am Dr. R. C. Richards III, and he would back me up. Buds father was a retired Congressman and well respected in this town. One day I was doing an odd job to get a little cash by mowing an overgrown lawn. I worked hard that day chopping down huge weeds and mowing the lawn. Then as I went into the screened in porch to knock on her kitchen door, a sheriff drove up and arrested me for trespassing. It was his mother's house and he did not care about the fact that I had just worked several hours on the yard.

He decided I was trespassing and carted me off to jail. I had no ID on me when I was being arrested, which was fortunate, so I told him my name is Dr. R. C. Richards III PhD. D, and dared him to call my dad. He called me a liar, (which was accurate I suppose) and promptly picked up the telephone and made the call. From the holding cell I could see the expressions on his face go sour, and I knew Bud was coming to my rescue. In just a few minutes the cell door opened and my dear old adopted father walked in and began to scold me in front of the officers. He said in loud voice as he grabbed me by the ear leading me out of captivity, "Damn it boy, I send you to school and buy you the books, but all you do is eat the paper! What's the matter with you!"

We got in the car while he was scolding me and drove off under the watchful eye of the cop that arrested me. When we turned the corner we laughed our butts off. Bud told me that the local police considered me dangerous and had targeted me. They wanted to put me on the chain gang. He suggested I lay low a few days to stay out of trouble, and took me to his daughter's river front estate. I could hide-out there for the week since they were on vacation to plan my next move. During that week the telephone rang and a lady said she needed a priest to come to the aid of her dying father. Now that is an interesting coincidence, it might have been a wrong number, but she reached the right person. I told her I would be there very soon. I grabbed my Golden Robe I got at the Fountain of the World, my Bible, and went to the address she gave me. They looked startled when I arrived with hair down to my shoulders, a full beard, and dressed like God; but they did invite me in.

The old man was on his deathbed, there was no doubt about that. I went to him and asked if he was ready to meet God. He told me he was not sure, so I said let us pray. I held his hand gently and told him to repeat the words to the sinners prayer, and be ready to be with Jesus for eternity. I asked his daughter if they had any bread and wine, but they had none. So I substituted crackers for the bread, and soda pop for wine. This was his last Holy Communion. I gave him a piece of the cracker and told him to eat this in remembrance of Jesus, which did. Then I gave him a sip of the soda representing the blood of Christ, he drank it. Then I blessed him in a Latin with words. "Dominisk Obiskbo tu espirito Adlibitum infinitus en Kristo Redemptor". Which roughly translates to, God bless your spirit with eternal liberty in the name of Christ the redeemer. Finally, I poured a small amount of his drinking water into the palm of my hand, prayed silently, sprinkled his head with the water and baptized him in the name of the Father, Son and Holy Ghost.

The man was ready to go, and so was I. But, before I could make it back to Bud's the cops arrested me again. It seems the man died within minutes after I left, and the lady called the police. She told them she thought I was impersonating a man of the cloth, and thought a real priest would have prayed for him to be well again. As far as she was concerned I murdered the guy by making him think he was going to die with my ritual. She was mad as hell and blamed me for this sudden death.

I guess the liver and lung disease had nothing to do with it. In my own mind I could see tomorrow's headline, Holy Communion Kills Retired Gentleman Phony Priest Held without Bail. I knew right then my mission to Daytona was complete, and it was time to go. Some friends bailed me out within an hour, and I went to Bud's house to pack my papers. Bud told me they were going to throw the book at me to make an example. I was very mad, and the weather suddenly changed from clear to dark and stormy. While I was walking along the river, contemplating my next move, a bolt of lightning struck the water very close. I could feel the electricity in my bare feet, and with this shock came a brilliant idea. I went back to the house and called the Daytona News Journal and told them I was Dr. R. C .Richards III, and that Reverend Haltom was walking along the Halifax River when lightning struck.

I told them the he was walking in the water when it hit, and has disappeared. Then I shaved off my beard, and trimmed my hair way back. I didn't even recognize myself. Word was traveling fast about my sudden death so I contacted a minister at the Disciples of Christ First Christian Church, and got permission to hold a memorial service. We had an evening service with about fifty people mourning the loss of the Hippie Priest. I put the guitar in front of the altar and gave my own eulogy. It was very sad and lots people cried. I was somewhat amused that no one even recognized me. I was standing there in front of them, my voice was still the same, and my gestures just as animated.

I left Daytona Beach shortly after the funeral service and headed north. George Harrison, Ringo Starr, and Bob Dylan were all going to play in a concert for Bangladesh. I felt compelled to make it to New York City, I put myself in God's Hands, and started walking. Georgia was on my mind, and not far from Daytona Beach, but with my new clean cut look it was actually harder to get a ride. I made it to Georgia and the man dropped me off at a roadside restaurant, gas station, bar and amazingly a local radio station. It took me by surprise when I walked into this little red neck establishment and the cowboy bartender greeted me with a big old southern howdy pardner.

I had become used to the persecution that accompanied my long hair and beard. It took a few seconds to realize the fact that I had radically changed my appearance. I smiled and said, "Howdy Pardner" right back and told him I was from Brackettville Texas, and I was on my way to Nashville to record some songs. I asked if he wanted to hear a tune or two. He said "Hell yeah, whip out that guitar and follow me." He led me to his radio station and interrupted the music to announce a live performance by a Nashville recording artist, Trey Haltom. After the interview, which never mentioned Daytona Beach, he turned the mike over and I just played my heart out for several songs. It went amazingly well, and after the broadcast he ordered up a couple of burgers, fries, and Budweisers. His hospitality was real, and for an old Georgia red neck he was all right.

The road north stretched out before me, and I thought I had to go aid the people of Bangladesh. It was a worthy cause, and I felt compelled to be a part of it. I sent Apple Records a tape, along with the Daytona News Journal clipping after writing them first requesting permission to submit some material. I also told them I believed they were the fulfillment of Revelations 9 and they were the locusts, with faces like men and hair like women, with power in their voices. I walked about five miles before my next ride. The fresh air and nice weather made the day a memorable one. Fortunately, a truck driver stopped when he saw me walking with the guitar over my shoulder. So I hopped in and he asked if I had been on the radio a short while ago. He was happy when I told him yes, and I was delighted to be on the road again. I played several songs as he took me all the way to the outskirts of Savannah, Georgia. We had a good time. He enjoyed the music, and I enjoyed company.

Next I caught a ride with some soldiers on leave that took me through South Carolina, North Carolina, and Virginia. They dropped me off near the state line in Maryland. Just as I was thinking about how great everything was going, a state police officer stopped and told me it was against the law to hitch hike in Maryland. So I told him I would walk across the damn state. He just grinned and said go ahead.

I walked for several hours and covered a lot of ground, then tried to lay down for a short rest under a shady tree. The same cop came along and harassed me again. No rest for the wicked I reckon, so I kept on walking until I reached the Chesapeake Bay Bridge. Once again that same officer stopped and informed me that it was illegal for a pedestrian to cross the bridge. I crossed the street to the gas station and a gentleman offered me a ride to the Annapolis. On the way there, he told me his friend the Chief of Police would allow me to rest overnight in a cell, at no charge.

I got out at the Annapolis Police Department and went to see the Chief. He was pretty cool and offered to take me to breakfast in the morning to his friend's restaurant. The Chief said I was the topic of the day over the police radio, and treated me nice. The restaurant owner was happy to meet me and made an awesome breakfast that really hit the spot. He told me about a friend who needed a live in helper for a few hours a day. The pay was a an apartment and two meals a day. I almost made it to the lady's house when a young couple invited me to their home for a, herbal smoke and a vegetarian meal. That sounded so good I had to make the detour.

Annapolis seemed friendly and a welcome change from that state trooper's attitude. In the morning I met the retired cook and found out she lived right next door to my friends. I moved in and worked about two hours every day, vacuuming halls, cleaning restrooms, and common places and doing I settled into my new digs, lovingly and thankful. The four-story brick house was built in the mid 1800's. It had character, charm, and history. I do believe Edgar Allen Poe visited this place, because I found an original Edgar Allen Poe book with his signature on the title page. It was a first edition of his collected works.

I wrote the Thought of 0-4-9 in just one night. It was a vision that took place I wrote it very rapidly. It was long and confusing. I really did not understand the significance of what I had written. I had been ordained for a few years, and still wrestling with what the Fountain of the World had laid on me. This rambling message was prophecy for the end times, but I had to make sense of it. I had to be able to present it in a rational and logical manner. This was very challenging.. What I saw in this vision was something beyond a dream. it was inter-dimensional and realistic. I saw human nature in its most ungodly form, as creatures from the dark side of existence. I saw more than I left in the final version, but I figured you would never believe it any way. This insight strengthened my convictions to serve the Lord God.

The Thought of 049

A thought in my head that is burning my mind
A thought that continues it goes undefined
A thought that is something or nothing at all
This thought I'm creating is simply a ball
It comes and it goes and it bothers me so
It's dark yet it glows and continues to grow
Then vanishes almost to nothing at all
Then appears to be something most gentle and small
Then out of the darkness it glimmers and shines
It spins like a spiral climbing its vine
Endlessly driving me out of my mind
My mind oh my mind my mind
What is this blasted thing in my head?
I am sure that it's lasted enough years to be dead
At least that is what my psychiatrist said
But what does he know of what dwells in my head
It's a spirit I'm certain having traveled through space
He's parked here I'm certain he hides in my face
I pull down my curtain and feel his embrace
I close now my eyelids and ask for God's grace
Darkness surrounds me a blanket of black
This demon astounds me he sneaks up from back
Then suddenly flashing he attacks from the rear
As something is crashing, he speaks in my ear
Crraaakk it's nostalgic how long can this last
Be back in a Sec I heard him say fast
I count the first second the next moment's past
He comes in the second moment at last
I gaze at his eyeball his brow and his lid
I have waited till nightfall to see what he did
I have listened most careful to all that he's said
Yet still I am fearful of losing my head
Come forth fine demon escape from my mind
For before long I will leave you behind
I will pay you no mention I will pay you no mind
For your convention is that of the blind

You're just a creation a parasite of my mind
You dwell in my thought and you're something much less
Than a penthouse for paupers creating a mess
A jovial chap you truly might be
Yet never a clap shall you hear from me
For applause is for beauty and claps a disease
That renders you helpless to crawl on your knees
Be gone now fine serpent flee from my sight
Begin to repent now I pray that you might
Before I avenge thee with all of my might
And crush you completely to oblivion's flight
I see know a fog on thy spectacle once clear
As you croak like a frog when a fly is not near
You are the least of a hog having ne'er shed a tear
And the most of a pig as you cry in your fear
You run like a dog from the master you fear
Farewell feathered demon fly well as a seaman
O'er land and by ocean and never to land
For I've sent you a cruising to a different land
Of nowhere or no one of nothing I've known
For it was within me, you first called home
Now you have left me I am here all alone
Solitude is joy that you've never known
For you are awkward and clumsy you can't stand alone
You are less than an idiot who has lost his own home
Like the patriot parrot that flew from its cage
In a moment irrational in a spirit of rage
Now you gawk for your cracker and cry for your feed
You scream and you pester yet no one takes heed
For you left your first master your feeder indeed
Now you bleed like a bleeder and always shall bleed
You're not but a beggar you do no good deed
I venture to say there is no one you need
Now demon or parrot or whatever you are
I know you're a spirit I know you've flown far
You're your own pilot that is all that you are
So vanish completely and never appear
For I am now certain it's only I that can hear
Your squawking and gawking and crying with fear
And certain you know your destruction is near
For I am the destroyer, the master you fear
For I am your creator your end is here, your enemy is fear
You are dying you're dying, you're dying my dear
Patriot pauper of a spirit stand clear
You are nay but a spirit you have never been here...

Sitting silently solo and lonely
Singing softly slowly and gently
Knowing only the songbird is lonely
Truth is all nothing is less
Love is more none the less
It is truly a ball as I recall
To not get an answer and still get a yes
Considering less could be quite a mess
Unless, unless the answer is yes
Yes of coarse could be much worse
And worthless of course
When said to be less than yes
Such as the bush that's beat around
Much as it's crushed into the ground
By the concrete feet so often found
Upon the streets where they are bound
To the jungle gods of jungle town
Of ass fault land and asphalt ground
Where mountainous pillars created by man
Topple and crumble at his command
Upon the hand of jungle man
I have seen this man I have heard him scream
I have seen his hand in a gory dream
Of gaudy goblins in soddy streams
Of murky water or so it seems
Yet, who remembers all that's seen
Upon the screen of a dream or in a dream serene
Entrapped between a laps of time in a time machine
And in the space of nothing more or nothing less
Than can be seen in this lapse of time in a time machine
People ask often if I'm joking'
And where I've been and what I'm smoking'
Or is that your number on that token
Or have you a card with your number written
049 Oh that's fine
Sorry to bother but the law is written
Enter in brother the boss is waitin'
In there sitting anticipatin' contemplatin'
Of where you've been while he's been waitin'
049 I hope you're fine for I know I am
For I now have been waiting' since then
it's a quarter to ten again
Where have you been since then?
And have you been drinking or is that gin
Well I have been nowhere since before then
So now we know that it is ten

but then again ten when
Did it begin at ten or was that a quarter
before it should end
Or do you understand or
misunderstand; it's but one big,
and one little hand
Knock off the nonsense you blithering fool
Have you your sixpence for you know the rule
For no pence or no sense is the mark of a fool
Purchase from me this bright golden rule
I have not a sixpence but I know your rule
I have taken it for no cents so now you're the fool
Hark the bells ringing, the butler is bringing
Some dinner for both of us fools
Please be partaking that which he's making
Was found in the hob goblins pool
It's murky and urky and looks like beef jerky
I am sure it was cooked in the pool
Thank you so kindly,but no thank you kindly
I would rather not eat if it's cool
For I must depart now and begin to start now
The end that is breaking my heart
It's such a pity, to live in this city
It's falling apart every day
While mountains are growing harvesting sowing
Crop after crop every day
And buildings are rumbling
tumbling crumbling
Falling apart every day
While jungle man's standing
Obeying the commanding
Ass fault god in his heart
Poof...

My name in this realm is 0-4-9. I saw a dimension where man was an insignificant being. God was not present in this place, and the main demonic being offered to sell me his golden rule. It was symbolic, and took many years to digest. I would be long gone from Annapolis before the Thought of 0-4-9 ever sunk into my conscience and became presentable to the public. In the meantime, I knew this beautiful community was only a rest stop on this long and winding road. I still needed to get to New York, and visit Apple Records. Paul McCartney just released his song Uncle Albert (Hands across the Ocean) and again I felt a kinship to these angels whom I have known in previous lifetimes. I played an informal concert at the Annapolis Hilton and raised some traveling cash for the next leg of my journey.

One of my first stops on the road to New York was Washington D.C. The place rocks at night, then gets down to business in the day. The night was chilly but I met a sweet young lady who offered me shelter. I didn't ask many questions and entertained her to he delight. The next morning I found my way to an underground newspaper office that had a bookstore and apartments for the editors and staff. Leonard Cohen was a senior editor and the clerk showed me the door where I could find him.

I walked in and found Leonard and a friend kibitzing, and boldly said "Attention!" I had on a Sargent Pepper Jacket decorated with medals I found in Annapolis. Leonard asked who I was and I informed him that I was indeed Sgt. Pepper. I had no idea that this room was actually his private apartment and I just barged in like that, but he understood after I explained how the bookstore clerk pointed to his door. I set down and played a few tunes for my favorite songwriter. He liked my guitar solo "The Dawn". He earnestly invited me back when I pass this way again. He was preparing to fly to Denver for a concert, and was short on time but truly wanted to jam. I would love to collaborate on a tune with Leonard, and hoped to cross paths again.

Getting to New York City was a short hop from Washington D C. In New York City at the street level I found a town packed with impersonal plebeians that grunted and snarled whenever I said hello, or good morning. What a cold place to be both spiritually, and physically. It was fall, and winter was not far off. I never was one to carry a jacket, or bedroll. My guitar and writings were there to help me along the way. I called my guitar Squalbuggie, which is the phonetic rendering of the Yiddish term for beetle. I never needed anything else, God was living up to His end of the bargain, and I was doing the best I could, considering the magnitude of the task He laid on me.

This was a metropolis with subways below and buildings that trying to reach a better atmosphere. The street level people were in high gear. Coming and going and who knows what else. I wandered around a while and met a run away that needed a place to rest her weary head. There was another fellow offering her a place to sleep with some strings attached. For her sake I remained with them both in the apartment of the young man. This spared her the obligation to give in to the guy's desires.

The next morning we left and I found a shelter for runaway teens. I convinced the young lady to seek assistance from the David Wilkerson Teen Ministry. Afterward I went to the Saint Vincent Du Paul Center and had a great breakfast. They gave me a nice jacket while I was there, and they let me call Pastor Fred at the First Baptist Church of Del Rio, Texas, where I started from.

Things were going well considering how far I traveled for an event that was already over. I worked my way to the New York office of Apple Records and went up to their suite. The receptionist, Robin, was so cute that I nearly fell in love. She told me the boys were all in England at the Abbey Road Studio, and was sorry to be the bearer of bad news. I smiled and told her that her news was not as bad as what I have to deliver. I wrote a note that foretold John Lennon's assassination in New York. I said that I expected it to happen within the next few years. Robin about fell over, and I told her that I was also sorry to have to be the bearer of bad news. I wanted to warn John so he would be cautious when in the city. This must have been as memorable a day for Robin as it was for me. I felt like I had made it rain cats and dogs on their parade instead of a little drizzle. I hoped they would understand that I had to tell them It was for the better for all concerned.

This brought to mind the day I visited the Charles Manson Family. Charlie and his followers received the death sentence and the family was in a state of grief. I solemnly promised them that they would all be spared the execution date and no one would harm a hair on their heads. Charlie and the girls do escape the gas chamber, but John Lennon meets an early demise. I guess the good die young and the wicked get no rest. Many people wanted Charlie to rest in peace.

New York City is humongous Metropolis, and it took a while to get used to. Luckily I was wearing a robe I acquired in New Jersey. I met a retired dancer in the city named Vincent Martinelli. He took me to NBC studios, and we went upstairs to the Joe Franklin set. the host of a daytime Television show and the man that discovered Barbara Streisand. Joe called his friend Dick Roffman to arrange for me to be on his program that same afternoon. It was Memorial Day and a special broadcast from Upstairs at the Downstairs was set as a remote broadcast for Dick and his guests. While waiting for the broadcast to begin, I met a bunch of men who liked my guitar so much they decided to keep it. The

cops could do nothing about it because I could not name or identify them. So I visited Dick Roffman's radio show and read a couple of poems from my book. I kept a hand made journal in a beautifully bound black book that I wrote a special dedication to Vincent Martenelli thanking him for opening so many doors. I called the book Ex Libra, and Old Man Murphy reared his ugly head and I had to backtrack to regroup. Without my guitar I was at quite a disadvantage as a musician, and suddenly I was put out of work. A quick call to my friend Pastor Fred in Del Rio, Texas, was all I needed to get some cash wired to me. Soon with cash in hand I hopped on a Greyhound Bus and headed south to Florida. Even though I had been recently eulogized by Dr. R. C. Richards III, in the Church of Christ in Daytona Beach, Florida.

On the way back to Texas I visited some ladies in Baltimore, Maryland. I stopped by there for a day of surfing St Peters burg's shoreline. It is always nice to spend a day with new acquaintances. I met the girl from St. Peters burg on the way north, and she invited me to drop by anytime. I loved her independence, and admired her success. She had a cozy little beach house, and the waves were pounding the shore. After a nice day of surfing, I decided to slip back into Daytona where I could borrow a few hundred dollars from the bank. I needed to finance my next guitar and was amazed the loan officer was so happy to oblige. He recognized me from the Daytona News Journal article, but did not know about the funeral. He just lent money to a known dead man and still got paid back.

Dan Hyde was a great friend, and was happy to know I had come back. His stepfather was also a friend of mine, and was the retired chief of police in Daytona. We all went to see an Apollo launch at Cape Canaveral from the Halifax River. We were on a large boat and were as close to the launch pad as we could possibly be. A photographer from Life magazine was on board and recorded the launch from the boat. When the rocket blasted off we could feel the heat wave as it blew by. We felt the energy it took to defy gravity. I was happy to see a clean lift-off, because I used to be inspector for the ground support electronics system at North American Aviation Rocketdyne, and had a personal sense of satisfaction knowing the engine and ground support system worked perfectly.

I went to work for Dan Hyde as a circuit design engineer and made a printed circuit board for his invention a digital meter reader that worked over the telephone lines. We worked a graveyard shift in Dan's lab, then sleep in till well after noon. The gadget worked very well, but would have put too many meter readers out of work, so the power company paid off Dan's boss who came up with the concept. Dan and I developed it in the Lab and were paid for the effort, but there was no future in manufacturing our little digital meter reading system. so we parted ways when I got on a bus, and headed to Kermit, to see my grandparents, Slim and Toletha Thorpe.

Nanny and Papa Slim lived in a small house with a little yard. It was very cool and Kermit was a one-light town in the middle of the oil patch. This was Tax Season, and Nanny had an Income Tax Service with clients that returned to every year. She did the books and taxes for some of her clients. We got busy and worked every day till late in the evening. This lasted until early in May, and I was in the right place to meet nearly everybody in town. Kermit is very close to Wink, the town where Roy Orbison grew up, and small enough to have a close knit community.

After a long dry spell I met a young opera student how had a voice like an angel. Ginger Schmidt was so sweet and innocent that she had a nun like quality. She was Southern Baptist, reborn and saved and we began to perform at her church We also played for the V F W on Memorial Day. She sang The Battle Hymn of the Republic so well the local newspaper covered our appearance.

It was not too long after Ginger and I began to date a deputy sheriff came to my house and ordered me to leave town. It seems he had a love interest in Ginger Schmidt, so one of us had to go. He was dead serious in his threat, and I was not amused. Slim was there and ordered him to leave having recognized the illegal nature of his visit. His brother was the retired Sheriff and we turned him in. Not long after, I heard on the news that he had taken a job in New Mexico as a police officer.

According to the story the man was fired for police brutality and wound up on the wrong side of the bars. I was delighted and Ginger was relieved, we knew God had His hand in these results. Ginger went east for college shortly after that,and I prepared for a trip to California. A vacation was overdue. I bought a Plymouth Fury, and fixed it with a two tone lacquer paint job, and a major tune up. It included a Police Car Interceptor Transmission, with a built in overdrive that felt like an afterburner kicking in. Nanny and I were done with all the Tax Returns, and needed a vacation. We set out for California, and I played my new Nielsen Eight Track tape with some of my favorite songs in stereo.

I visited my folks for little bit, then went to Venice Beach to go to the ISKCON Temple we call New Dwarka, I was excited to get back to the place and spend some time in devotion, and fellowship with my God Brothers. I missed them so much during my journey across the country and back, The best thing of all was to be in the presence of Sri Krishna and be able to chant some rounds of the Maha Mantra, Hare Krishna Hare Krishna Krishna Krishna Hare Hare Hare Rama Hare Rama Rama Rama Hare Hare. Krishna blessed me and I was ecstatic. He was with me all the way to New York and back. God directed my travels, every step of the way, and I never let him out of my mind.

I wish I could pinpoint the exact time I was at New Dwarka, the ISKCON Temple in East LA. The first time I arrived there I had picked up a hitch hiking devotee in San Francisco and I drove him to the temple near Venice Beach. I stayed with them for a while to learn about Krishna, and find out what made the devotees so pleasant to be around. It was our common love for the Lord Sri Krishna. I was already ordained High Priest of the Order of Melchizedek. The brothers and Sisters at the Monastery in Box Canyon were followers of Melchizedek, who called Himself Krishna Venta. We believed He was an incarnation of the same God the Hare Krishna Devotees worshiped, and I was the friend of Krishna forever after that.

After the first trip across the states and back to California, I stayed for awhile in the New Dwarka Temple. I believe it was then that George Harrison made his way to the temple and chanted with us for a while. He met with Prabhupada on a day while I was chanting on the streets of LA devotees doing Hare Namn during my first stay in 1967. From there I continued on the journey God sent me on. Several years passed, For a while I was married then later I was free to go on the road again.

One of the greatest accomplishments in my life was to start the movement here in Phoenix when I brought ISKCON to town. I ran into a devotee at the zoo one day; he was in street clothes and doing some sort of fund raising for the ISKCON Temple and Vegetarian Restaurant in Tucson. I asked him if he would help bring a temple here to Phoenix, and he agreed to help. It wasn't long until we got the building in Chandler, AZ, and for the first year I stayed there as a devotee, chanted daily and helped build the inside of the ISKCON Temple, and landscape and garden outside. We had no Guru available on-site, so after one year I was initiated by a senior devotee who was born in an ISKCON Hare Krishna Temple. He gave me the name Madhavendra Puri, which translates from Sanskrit to "The Friend of Krishna, while Puri means Spiritual Master.

This came at quite a cost however because the fundamentalist Christian Church my mom, sister, and other family members belonged to were quite opposed to this temple. They believed Prabhupada was a crazy old man from India who made up this false religion where we offer food to idols and are brain washed by the monotonous repetition of our Hare Krishna mantra. "Hare Krishna Hare Krishna Krishna Krishna Hare Hare Hare Rama Hare Rama Rama Rama Hare Hare"

The Fundamentalist Christians professed that anybody who ate the food offered to these idols would be cast into hell, and that there was no redemption after taking prashadam, our vegetarian cuisine. So in order to keep my children spiritually safe, they conjured up a plan to declare my wife Kitty and I insane and too incompetent to care for our children. The CPS took away my kids, and I was tossed in a mental hospital, declared seriously mentally ill, and the children were allowed to be adopted by families handpicked by these Christian Zealots.

It was just about sixteen years before I saw my four children again. When they came of age they all returned to me with resentment towards the government, Fundamental Christians, the courts, prosecutors, and most of all the CPS. There will be a lot of condemnation coming down when God returns, and for them I feel no great sorrow or loss. Good riddance to Edith Buyers, the Wicked CPS Lady, and all glories to Sirla Prabhupada my dearest Spiritual Master. My Guru and Spiritual Master today, in July of 2014, is His Holiness Krishna Mangala Swami, a loving saint and Godly person. He is so dear to me because I can feel His Divine Presence from halfway around the world, and I can hardly wait to arrive in India very soon to spend the rest of my life is spiritual bliss next to my beloved Guru, Krishna Mangala Swami. ISKCON is the greatest organization this world has ever seen, and we will save the world with our love. Hare Krishna.

Bishop Asaiah ordained me in 1966 High Priest

Krishna Venta was Melchizedek always has been

This was in 1966 at the Fountain of the World

Who ever arrested Krishna is in trouble

Fountain of the World Monastery 585 Box Canyon Road, Box Canyon, California

This i where we met for services and Saturday Night Jam Sessions. Musicians came from all over Southern California to bed a part of these wonderful gatherings. We believed in Peace and Love. and often got young me their draft deferment as a conscientious objector because we believed in the Ten Commandments, and Thou Shall Not Kill meant not to go to war.

Charles Manson and his "Family" were regular visitors, and they were there when I gave a short sermon on Revelations 9, proclaiming the Beatles were the fulfillment of the prophesy of the locusts with faces like men and hair like women, with power in their voices, breast plates of steel, with tails that sting like a scorpion. (their electric guitars). Charlie must have figured that he was Abaddon, the King of the Beatles, also called the destroyer, he mixed his thoughts of Helter Skelter with that and the rest is history. After the trial and when they all received the death penalty, I made a bold prophesy that they would never harm a hair on any of their heads.

Bhaktivendenta Cultural Center, 100 South Weber, Chandler, Arizona

Temple Alter ISKCON Phoenix

It once was a Buddhist Martial Arts academy, but we transformed it into a Temple for Krishna

We Dwell in the Secret Place, by Trey Haltom, BMI

We were homeless when we got here, We were not homeless for too long
For the Angels that surround us kept us going ever strong
A midst the hatred of our neighbors who have done my loved on wrong
But the memory of their wickedness dissipates into a song

    For we will dwell in the secret place beneath the feathers of His wings
    Under the Shadow of the Almighty we will abide as refugees
    You will know the Lords our fortress, Mighty Angels care for us
    In our homes and in our strongholds, In God's Love we're strong and bold

Our eyes alone will soon behold all the wicked's just rewards
As we trample on the Lyons, and the adders young and old
And never shall we fear or sweat the terror of the night
Or the arrows of the day as they pass us in swift flight
Nor the pestilence that walks a midst the darkness of the night
And the destruction of the cities they have wasted in daylight

    For we will dwell in the secret place beneath the feathers of His wings
    Under the Shadow of the Almighty we will abide as refugees
    You will know the Lords our fortress, Mighty Angels care for us
    In our homes and in our strongholds, in God's love we're strong and bold

A thousand to my side shall fall ten thousand to my right
No evil will befall me the Almighty is my might
Lest I dash my feet into a stone, and stumble in His sight
Or step into a Fowler's snare that can never hold me tight

    For we will dwell in the secret place beneath the feathers of His wings
    Under the Shadow of the Almighty we will abide as refugees
    You will know the Lords our fortress, Mighty Angels care for us
    In our homes and in our strongholds, in God's love we're strong and bold

My life will surely be eternal, my salvation is assured
I am covered by His feathers, not an Angel's or a bird
For it is God who is my fortress,and He shelters me
In troubled times I call on Him and then he answers me

    For we will dwell in the secret place beneath the feathers of His wings
    Under the Shadow of the Almighty we will abide as refugees
    You will know the Lords our fortress, Mighty Angels care for us
    In our homes and in our strongholds, in God's love we're strong and bold

The Wicked CPS Lady

My four children were taken away by Child Protective Services just because I started the Hare Krishna Movement in Phoenix. One fateful day in 1997 I saw a man standing by the entrance of the Phoenix Zoo selling funny bumper stickers. I stopped to talk with him, and found out he was actually a Devotee and president of the Tucson ISKCON Temple. So I invited devotees from Tucson to come to Phoenix and help start a local ISKCON facility.

We started out visiting homes of local families that came here from India and put on a Kirtan service and chanted the Hare Krishna mantra. Word spread and the groups grew larger each week. Soon we managed to buy a 7,000 square foot building in Chandler, and within one year we transformed an empty building into a beautiful temple and altar for Krishna. We serve Lord Krishna daily with a congregation of immigrants from India, Many of these people are highly skilled computer technicians, engineers, and software developers. All of the ISKCON Temple Devotees are respected by residents and government officials alike. That includes several town officials from Chandler, the mayor, and our own governor Jan Brewer.

Bhaktivedanta Cultural Center in1996 ISKCON Phoenix

Meanwhile, the ministers from Faith Evangelical Free Church in Tempe were adamantly opposed to us building this temple. They told my sister and mother who were members of their church that if the kids ever ate the food we served, they would be doomed to hell for eternity. They said there would be no avenue for redemption, and preached from the pulpit that it was an unpardonable sin of blasphemy to eat the food that has been offered to false idols.

This is the food that the Faith Evangelical Free Church believed would doom my children to hell for eternity, without any hope for redemption, because eating this constitutes the unforgivable sin of blasphemy.

This was my son Joshua at 4 years old writing his own original songs.
WATCH OUT WORLD...

Here come Old Flattop

They acted swiftly and managed to get me fired from the job where I had been promoted to a managers position. They told the owner I needed to be at the emergency psychiatric service center by five so I wouldn't have to wait for my medication. It took the company three days to find an excuse to fire me. Then my sister and mom took over the house I was buying and sold it out from under me, They kept the proceeds for themselves, telling me they sold it at a loss.

They then filed the documents necessary to have my wife and I committed and put under court ordered treatment for a year. My wife was suffering acute diabetes high sugar levels at that time   and was just out of the intensive care unit the day the CPS came by. She was in bad shape, and it made her seem a little crazy, so the hauled her away. The police came to my house on Christmas Eve and took me away in handcuffs, then locked me in a mental ward. I believe the timing was meant to be that very day, because they had me pegged as the Antichrist, and timed it so to please God.

The most absurd claim they made during all of this was that we had nailed vegetables to the wall and forced our children to worship them. For that reason they had the children placed by CPS with several families and made wards of the court. The state government paid these foster parents very well for their service.

The fact is, according to the Constitution, if I really did want to nail vegetables to the wall and have my children to worship them, I have the constitutional right to do just that. Freedom of religion is one of the main reasons the first boat load of Pilgrims landed on the shores of what would soon become the United States of America.

At the trial the judge was biased, and the prosecutor lied several times. When I pointed this out to my court appointed attorney, he said that was common since prosecutors were not under oath. I spoke up and told the judge I wanted to hire a private attorney and he replied, "You can get any attorney you want, but it won't do you any good in this court."

Two of my children were adopted and never allowed to contact us until they turned eighteen years old. One daughter was raised by my mom and sister until she left their home with her boyfriend when at sixteen and pregnant. My oldest son was placed in several state run group homes and forced to take a experimental drugs, including psychotropic medication used to keep the seriously mentally ill patients under sedation. In these medical tests they subjected him to a variety of mind control drugs, and recorded his reactions. Basically they treated my son just I Ike a laboratory rat.

Since his release from the Child Protective Service court ordered hold on him, he was sent to live with me and my wife in Northern California It was late in December, and he arrived nearly barefoot and with no warm clothes. He has not been able to hold down a job for any length of time, and it has been this way during his entire life adult life.   .

One reason for his constant state of unemployment is he has very little work experience and no on the job training. He never graduated from High School because they moved him around the state constantly, and he was denied a decent education due to the CPS workers lack of concern.

None of my children have a normal opportunity to succeed, because of the way they were raised. There was no spiritual development or true love for the children from these foster and adoptive parents. The foster parents didn't care about that aspect of life, with the exception of one daughter who attended church regularly. The other foster parents had no regard for the souls of these children because it had nothing to do with the hundreds of dollars they received each month, and the child's spiritual development was not a requirement of the agency regulating the foster parenting program.

One daughter works as an exotic dancer, while the other is just loose and known to sleep around. She had an infant son that was taken away from her by the CPS when he was a tiny infant. They had absolutely no reason to remove this child from her, but the wicked CPS lady just did it because she could. I think this woman likes inflicting pain and agony on to loving parents whose lives she has ruined.

Then to add insult to injury, the CPS lady handed the baby over to the ex- husband who just got out the Navy Brig after being found guilty of aggravated assault and child endangerment. The fetus was nearly full term in my daughter's womb during the vicious attack. He was dishonorably discharged after serving his prison sentence. The man grievously sinned and injured my youngest daughter but got custody of the child. He and that wicked bureaucrat from the Child Protective Services will get their just reward soon. God will not tolerate such utter disregard for the welfare of His children. This is God's word along with the everyday repercussions of Karma.

Speaking of Karma, this all happened at the same time the I had just spent an entire year as a devotee in the ISKCON Temple that I had started, We didn't have a Guru on site, so I was informally initiated by my God Brother, Bhakta Ra, and given the ISKCON Initiated name, Madhavendra Puri, We all know that means the friend of Krishna, and Spiritual Master. The name is perfect for me because I really am Madhavendra Puri, now.

It was then a senior devotee, Sabuda Krishna Das asked me if I ever considered becoming a Guru. Of course I had, because I was ordained High Priest of the Order of Melchizedek when I first associated with and lived in the Los Angeles Temple, New Dwarka, in 1966 - 1967. So, I told Sabuda Krishna Das that I would gladly accept karmic responsibility for all of ISKCON. Then I went into my room, and climbed a ladder to get something from the loft. When I did the ladder slipped and I fell right on the two by four strut and broke 6 ribs, three of them were compound fractures and it was extremely painful.

When I got to the hospital the X Ray technician wanted me to be closer to the screen, so he pushed me into the machine and punctured my lungs. I was there three days, and I had enough of their malpractice, and rinsed off my temple clothes, pulled out the catheter, and left the hospital. I wasn't worried, God wounded me for taking on all that karma, and He will make it better.

I left Arizona with the thousand new CDs I had just published called Starry Eyed by R. Paige, and headed to Portola, California.

Hare Krishna Hare Krishna Krishna Krishna Hare Hare
Hare Rama Hare Rama Rama Rama Hare Hare

All Glories to Sirila Prabupada

Madhavendra Puri ISKCON Phoenix 1996

Madhavendra Puri with God Daughter Sondra and the troupe

Trey & Shoba

Colonel Pepper

Damadora by Madhavendra Puri

namäméçvaraàm sac-cid-änanda-rüpaàm

lasat-kuëòalaà gokule bhräjamanam

yaçodä-bhiyolükhaläd dhävamänaà

parämáñöam atyantato drutya gopyä
  Hare Hare Krishna
  Krishna Krishna
  Hare Hare

varam deva mokṣam na mokṣāvadhim vā

na canyam vṛṇe 'ham vareṣād apīha

idam te vapur nātha gopāla-bālam

sadā me manasy āvirāstām kim anyaiḥ
  Hare Hare Rama
  Rama Rama
  Hare Hare

namo deva dāmodarānanta viṣṇo

prasīda prabho duḥkha-jālābdhi-magnam

kṛpā-dṛṣṭi-vṛṣṭyāti-dīnam batānu

gṛhāṇeṣa mām ajñam edhy akṣi-dṛśyaḥ
  Hare Hare Krishna
  Krishna Krishna Hare Hare
  Hare Hare Rama
  Rama Rama Hare Hare

The Two Witnesses

There is a bit of information I have been withholding. I have known this for nearly 50 years, and have not mentioned it to any one. When I was at the Fountain of the World, in Box Canyon, California (GOOGLE THIS) and about to be ordained High Priest at the age of 19, they first told me I was the Messiah, and I asked them how am I supposed to save the world, and they said don't worry, you will figure it out. Well it rook nearly 50 years to do that, but I did figure it out, so every thing is in place to ready to go. The fulfillment of all prophesies is under way, and we have a major role in this effort.

You and I are the two witnesses mentioned in Revelations 11. We will travel the globe, dressed in sack cloth, our saffron robes, as we go to every country bringing the path to world peace to the heads of state in each nation. This will take 3 1/2 years to accomplish. exactly 1,240 days from the beginning to the bitter end. I say bitter end because our last stop will be in Iraq, the cradle of civilization, and our death bed. We will be shot dead on the streets of Iraq, on prime time TV, Live so to speak. Our devotees will surround our lifeless bodies, and protect us from even being touched by the ravenous beasts that would like to eat our livers as a sign of total defeat. Much of the world will celebrate our death, and rejoice that the two prophets are silenced once and for all. The party will last for three and a half days, while we descend into hell to deposit the sins we have taken karmic responsibility for. You for your devotees, including me, an I for all of ISKCON, which I accepted responsibility for about 15 years ago, in my own temple in Chandler

Now the good news is that after exactly three and a half days of lying dead in the street, with around the clock video tape being broadcast worldwide, A shout will come from out of the clouds, and both Jesus and Sri Krishna will tell us to rise and come up hither, This is the great day of judgment. and we have the privilege to take part is this affair Krishna Mangala Swami. Like I mentioned in the song from Psalms 91, We Dwell in The Secret Place, Our eyes alone will soon behold all the wicked's just reward.

After that we will have a thousand year life to bring this planet up to par for the likes of Krishna, and the top deities that we have so diligently been serving all these lifetimes. The thing I never mentioned to anybody is that I am Arjuna, and I did indeed write the Song of God , and many parts of the Bible too. My new work is both Christian and Krishna Conscious, The New Psalms ~ The Songs of God. (That was a little hint I was letting you have all along.)

With Oceans of Love

Madhavendra Puri

AKA Rev. Trey Haltom

George Harrison Memorial Garden at New Dwarka ISKCON LA

Memorial Garden Poster

I drove this bus, The Vicuntha Express, each week to ASU and pick up students for services

Times Done Changed

By, Colonel O. W. Pepper with music by Bob Dylan

There is a fury in my soul that just will not cease

There is an anger in my mind cause there just ain't no peace

I see the whole world, and it is going quite mad

I sit here each day, and I am growing quite sad

There is a battle outside, and it's coming here soon

So I guess what we need is a new marching tune

Like the Battle Hymn sang to the enemy in blue

The Star Spangled Banner, it never will do

When the United States is divided in two

And it's all over now my sweet baby blue

Our leaders have brought us again into war

And diverted our minds from what happened before

Iraq ain't no sweat, so why all the fuss

The damned old Chinese have just conquered us

There is a battle outside, and it is coming here soon

So I guess what we need is a new marching tune

Like the Battle Hymn sang to the enemy in blue

The Star Spangled Banner, it never will do

When the United States is divided in two

And it's all over now my sweet baby blue

It is time that we took us some kings and queens down

From the highest of places to beneath the ground

Hang all of them mothers right out in plain view

Do unto them others, before they do it to you

There is a battle outside, and it is coming here soon

So I guess what we need is a new marching tune

Like the Battle Hymn sang to the enemy in blue

The Star Spangled Banner, it never will do

When the United States is divided in two

And it's all over now my sweet baby blue

I wrote this song near the end of the Clinton years. He was embroiled in the Lewinsky scandal, and it seems he started up a bombing session over Iraq, practically unprovoked. It looked like Clinton was trying to divert the news media from his impeachment, and a leave office a hero. I told a co-worker once, that he would be the last president we ever elect. Sure enough, the next election came and the authorities selected the winner; the voters had little to do with it, other than display the fact that this nation is divided in two. Our new fearless leader is a hawk, and seems to enjoy the role of Commander in Chief. The Lord moves in mysterious ways, and makes arrangements continuously.

Now Iraq is in our sights again; China has expressed support for the attack on Afghanistan, under the guise of the War on Terrorism. How they react to the next phase of this battle is open to speculation. My best guess is that China will be less vocal in their support. We are on the road to Armageddon, and there is no turning back. Iraq has been supportive of the terrorists, as they were tools of revenge for Saddam Hussein. When Clinton tried to assemble a coalition of allies for his later attack, there was very little support, and the effort fizzled. In his last days in office, there was a flurry of visits to communist regimes such as North Korea, China, and other European nations. Making China a favored trade nation was a sell out, nothing less. What we do not know is the scary part. China received technical advances with guidance system electronics that help their atomic warhead delivery systems. With the technology they received, China is able to send intercontinental ballistic missiles globally, with pinpoint accuracy. Thanks Bill!

In order to fulfill all prophesy, and bring Gods harvest about; it is necessary for the world to recognize what has already been fulfilled. As God's messenger, my duty is to proclaim the fall of Babylon, from within the temple. Having done so on 9/11, I can carry out the final mission of bringing unity to all who believe in the living God, for anything less than a true communion with the creator of this universe is idolatry. Therefore, I will begin with the simple message that Babylon has fallen. It fell dramatically on my own father's birthday, September 11. The Twin Towers of the World Trade Center housed the merchants described in the 18th chapter of Revelations.

Here is where we stand today, at a point when time should be no more. We can bring about the total annihilation, or find a peaceful solution. The choice is simple, and so is the solution. The truth is often stranger than fiction, according to the cliche, and this truth is what I intend to present in The Book of Completion.

The prophesies of Daniel and Saint John the Divine may well have been written by the same person, in different times. The Book of Revelations describes these end times in a manner that parallels Daniel's narration of his vision. To read it literally, and digest the imagery feeds our soul as if we had eaten the words. In the eighth through the eleventh verse of Revelations 10, John writes:

And the voice which I heard from heaven spake unto me again, and said, Go and take the little book which is open in the hand of the angel which stands upon the sea and upon the earth. And I went unto the angel, and said unto him, give me the little book. And he said unto me, Take it and eat it up; and it shall make thy belly bitter, but it shall in thy mouth be as sweet as honey. And I took the little book out of the angel's hand and ate it up; and it was in my mouth as sweet as honey; and as soon as I had eaten it, my belly was bitter. And he said unto me, Thou must prophesy again before many peoples, and nations, and tongues, and kings.

This is a mystery to many; but it shows me that John understood he would be returning to this world to prophesy again. As it was, he wrote the Revelations in the twilight of his days. John was a fully realized soul even when he came as an apostle of Christ, and would be angelic in the end times. We entertain angels unaware, and angels entertain in the same fashion. The locusts with faces like men and the hair of women are angels, according to what John wrote in the ninth chapter of Revelations. I believe John knew he would be in that number (Number 9), when the saints come marching in. We all are here, and must remain, as this generation will not pass until all these things are fulfilled, according to Jesus, our Lord and Master. We are the last generation. Blessed are those that die in these days, is written in Revelations 14 (the chapter that so clearly describes the Hare Krishna Movement). We are presently at a point of fulfillment so near completion that everyone should read this passage carefully. Revelations 14:1-5

"And I looked, and, lo, a Lamb stood on the mount Zion, and with him a hundred and forty and four thousand, having His father's name written on their foreheads. And I heard a voice from heaven, as the voice of many waters, and as a voice of a great thunder: and I heard the voice of harpist harping with their harps: And they sung as it were a new song before the throne, and before the four beasts, and the elders: and no man could learn that song but the hundred and forty and four thousand, which were redeemed from the earth. These are they which were not defiled with women; for they are virgins. These are they which follow the Lamb wither soever He goes. These were redeemed from among men, being the first fruits unto God and to the Lamb. And in their mouth was found no guile: for they are without fault before the throne of God."

Considering we are in the end times; it must be that a group of individuals united in a belief in God, would even write the name of God on their foreheads. So look around and list all of the religious organizations around the world that fit the list of requirements mentioned in this scripture. They also must be the first fruits of God, so the religion must date back thousands of years, at least. ISKCON has that number of devoted members, plus a few.

In the next few passages, the angel described has already fulfilled his mission. His Divine Grace A. C. Bhaktivedanta Swami Prabhupada, Founder of the International Society for Krishna Consciousness (ISKCON) translated the everlasting gospel when he published the Srimad Bhagavatam and Bhagavad-Gita As It Is. The Song of God is the translation of the title, Bhagavad-Gita. In the Hare Krishna temple, we sing songs written in Sanskrit; some of these date back 5,000 years, and some are more recent. These are truly the songs mentioned in Revelations 14 verse 3. In the entire world, nothing else comes close to this manifestation of the fulfillment of this prophecy, because when you sing these songs, you understand the relationship between God and His first fruits. Krishna is the Supreme Personality of Godhead, and revealed this to the world in that song.

His Divine Grace A. C. Bhaktivedanta Swami Prabhupada once said, "Jesus is our guru". Jesus is the ultimate guru. He can deliver us from our sins even after His crucifixion, from His place at the right hand of the Father. A living spiritual master, or guru, can only accept the karmic responsibility of his disciples while on this earth, during his own lifetime. Therefore, all devotees of Prabhupada are servants of Sri Krishna and Jesus Christ, by proxy, thanks to ISKCON Founder, His Divine Grace A. C. Bhaktivedanta Swami Prabhupada. Hari Bol Revelations 14:6-7

"And I saw another angel fly in the midst of heaven, having the everlasting gospel to preach unto all them that dwell on the earth, and to every nation, and kindred, and tongue, and people, Saying in a loud voice, Fear God, and give glory to Him; for the hour of His judgment is come: and worship him that made heaven, and earth, and the sea, and the fountains of water". His Divine Grace A. C. Bhaktivedanta Swami Prabhupada flew all over this world doing exactly what this verse describes. He came to America, and brought us the everlasting gospel, that has outlived all forms of scripture known to mankind. The Sanskrit language was the original language of this planet, before the fall of the tower of Babylon, when we all spoke one tongue.

In the next verse, another angel follows His Divine Grace A. C. Bhaktivedanta Swami Prabhupada. The second angel announces that Babylon has fallen. This is now fulfilled in me, as we read: Revelations 14:8. I was in the Temple when the jets crashed into the Twin Towers, and I said Babylon has Fallen, and then a second time when the second tower collapsed.

"And there followed another angel, saying, Babylon is fallen, is fallen, that great city, because she made all nations drink of the wine of the wrath of her fornication". Having completed this, we can all expect the next angel to fulfill the prophesy written in verses nine through twelve, which is described as rewarding to the saints, while quite destructive to those who persist in idolatry. This is the patience of the saints, according to Revelations 14 verses nine through twelve: Revelations 14:9-12

"And the third angel followed them, saying with a loud voice, If any man worship the beast and his image, and receive his mark in his forehead, or in his hand, The same shall drink of the wine of the wrath of God, which is poured out without mixture into the cup of His indignation; and he shall be tormented with fire and brimstone in the presence of his holy angels, and in the presence of the Lamb; and the smoke of their torment ascends up forever and ever: and they have no rest day or night, who worship the beast and his image, and whosoever receives the mark of his name.

Here is the patience of the saints: here are they that keep the commandments of God and the faith of Jesus". What the next angel will say may be hard to swallow, but to those who are enjoying the message, it is quite satisfying. The key to this situation determines where you stand with God. It all depends on whether or not you are worshiping the beast and his image, or worshiping the creator of this universe, and living God. The difference is easy to recognize by using the commandments of God as a measure. By obeying the commandments, one falls into the better category, while the acts of the other reveal themselves in wicked ways. Each side has its own reward, and all men have the same choice to make: and that is whom do we serve God or the beast? This is definitely worthy of consideration because the stakes are so high, and you pay this price with your soul. Personally, I hope we all chose the same living God.

The good news is that God is not as particular as one may believe, concerning what we call Him. When God appeared as the burning bush to Moses, He said, "I am that I am". Krishna said about the same thing to Arjuna. ISKCON chants, "Hare Krishna Hare Krishna Krishna Krishna Hare Hare Hare Rama Hare Rama Rama Rama Hare Hare": We could also sing, "Praise God Praise God Oh God Oh God I'll serve you Lord I'll serve you Lord Oh Lord Oh Lord", it's the same meaning either way.

Jesus said that no man comes unto the Father except through me. I believe that, but that does not mean a devotee on his way to heaven will run into Jesus and be sent to hell. No way, Jesus would point the way to the Father. Jesus even quoted David's Psalm and said, "The Lord said unto my Lord, sit at my right hand, and I will make thy enemies a footstool". Have you ever wondered what Lord said this unto which Lord? The next passage in the Book of Revelations 14 verse 13 through 20 describes the harvest. The next angel rides in on a white cloud, has a crown on his head, and is like unto the Son of man. He will thrust his sickle into the earth when the angel of the temple calls on him to reap His harvest: Revelations 14: 13-16.

And I heard a voice from heaven saying unto me, Write, Blessed are the dead which die in the Lord from henceforth: Yea, saith the Spirit, that they may rest from their labors; and their works do follow them. And I looked and behold a white cloud, an upon the cloud one sat like unto the Son of Man, having on his head a golden crown, and in his hand a sharp sickle. And another angel came out of the temple, crying with a loud voice to him that sat on the cloud, Thrust in thy sickle, and reap; for the time has come for thee to reap, for the harvest of the earth is ripe. And he that sat on the cloud thrust in his sickle on the earth; and the earth was reaped. The fulfillment of this prophesy is imminent, aad we will enjoy the rewards in this lifetime.

This is the end of time, as we know it. This planet where man has the illusion that time is an endless commodity, comes to grip with the superior reality that it is finite, because; just as it had a beginning, it also must have an end. Here we have a clue that those who die in the Lord from now on will find rest from their labors, and their works follow them. This is good, because the finer things in life continue in this superior level of existence where time is immaterial. The Bhagavad-Gita confirms this, and here is where the patience of the saints pays off. The exact timing of these events coincides with the battle of Armageddon, the inevitable wrath of God, where blood flows to the height of the horse's bridal, in a space of what some consider the Holy Land, (200 square miles).

This also coincides with the conclusion of the testimony of the two witnesses mentioned in Revelations 11, and comes three and a half days after they are shot. I volunteered for this detail fifty years ago, and am ready to begin this three and a half-year journey with my appointed sidekick, as soon as the Antichrist rears his ugly head. He is there in the revived Roman Empire we call the European Union. His Mark is the common currency; the Beast is the name of the computer that details all transactions of this electronic fund. The Mark is the only currency that does not have a coin or bill, but is legal tender just the same. The United Nations sponsors the New World Order, and our politicians have signed on to this cause. These who cry "Peace. Peace", then sudden destruction falls on them. Peace in Israel is impossible without the messiah.

Before the fulfillment of these Revelations, and the harvest of the earth that is the Judgment Day, some prophecies remain unfulfilled. The one who sits on the cloud mentioned in this 14th chapter of Revelations, is made like unto the Son of Man. This leads to speculation that this could be either Jesus Christ or someone quite like Him. In Hebrews 7, a similar passage describes Melchizedek being made like unto the Son of God. As High Priest of the Order of Melchizedek, or the similitude of it, my intention is to show that Melchizedek is a manifestation of Krishna, the everlasting God in the form of a man. I am His High Priest, and have been for a long time, Hebrews 7:1-10.

For this Melchizedek, King of Salem, priest of the most high God, who met Abraham returning from the slaughter of the kings; and blessed him; To whom also Abraham gave a tenth part of all; first being by interpretation King of righteousness, and after that also King of Salem, which is King of peace; Without father, without mother, without descent, having neither beginning of days, nor end of life; but made like unto the Son of God; abides a priest continually. Now consider how great this man was, unto whom even the patriarch Abraham gave a tenth of the spoils. And verily they that are the sons of Levi, who receive the office of priesthood, have a commandment to take tithes of the people according to the law, that is, of their brethren, though they come out of the loins of Abraham: But he who's descent is not counted from them received tithes of Abraham, and blessed him that had the promises. And without all contradiction, the less is blessed of the better. And here men that die receive tithes; but there he receives them, of whom it is witnessed that he lives. And as I may so say, Levi also, who received tithes, paid tithes in Abraham. For he was yet in the loins of his father, when Melchizedek met him.

This is the most profound passage in the Book of Hebrews. Even the Rev. Mathew Henry, was perplexed over who Melchizedek was. His best guess was that God intended this to be a mystery, and expected it to remain until a generation in the future. He also thought Melchizedek might be a type of Christ, if not even Christ himself, or perhaps one of the sons of Noah. The later would likely be wrong, because he had no beginning, nor end of time. That leaves out being human, and narrows the prospects down to one made like Christ; which would be the Father, or the Holy Ghost, or perhaps an angel of the highest order.

Melchizedek was priest of the "Most High God", at the time of Abraham, and the common name of that most high God then was Krishna. Melchizedek would have to be the most God like human ever to rule over a kingdom on this planet. Who else could make that claim, except Krishna? According to Hebrews 7, Levi also paid tithes through Abraham, and that Melchizedek met him while he was yet in the loins of his father. This association could only have been during a previous life. All of the descendants of Abraham have had previous lives. The High Priest of the Order of Melchizedek supersedes the Levitical priesthood, and is their messiah.

Jesus fulfilled the prophecies of the Savior when He died on the cross, and arose again in three days. I have the task of carrying on the mission from the ground level, while Jesus and God tarry a little longer on the throne. The Holy Spirit is the connecting force that unites us. This body is my temple, and the Holy Spirit dwells within this living altar to God the Father. I have the mind of Christ, and the body of a man who lives to serve the Lord. We will finish the work laid out for us by the prophets.

This is the period of the great tribulation. We are at war on two fronts, one abroad, the other at home. The War on Terrorism is a responsibility the government of the United States of America has to grapple with as the utmost priority. The other war, the "War on Drugs", continues on multiple fronts simultaneously. The police state mentality forced on society exists to groom them for total domination. The Federal Government is our effectual shepherd, by design. It is important for this entity to respect the individual and treat them properly. To intimidate them with force and cruelty is wrong and dividing. (Ezekiel 34)

Melchizedek aka Krishna Venta at the Fountain of the World , Box Canyon, California

Everybody Must Get Stoned..

Everybody must get stoned... Bob Dylan sang those words. but what does God have to say about that? Have you ever pondered that? Well I have, and this is what I know to be true. Allow me to introduce my selves to you. That is not a typo either. Of coarse you know I am Trey Haltom, and I love all of my connections very much. As a singer and Songwriter I am well known as Colonel Oliver Wimbleton Pepper IV BMI , and rank number 4 in Arizona on

https://www.reverbnation/colonelpepper

please visit this page and become a fan. Fan Club Membership has it's rewards. Finally I am known as Madhavendra Puri in India as a Spiritual Master and High Priest of the Order of Melchizedek. I believe there is no one on this planet closer to God than me, that's impossible because Jesus said "There are none righteous, no not one; for all have sinned and came short of the Glory of God.

So let's look at the question again who must get stoned? Bob Dylan and I say everybody must get stoned! What does God say, you may wonder.. Let's ask Madhavendra Puri. he's the High Priest.

See Genesis 1 verse 27 through 31

I would highlight verse 29   And God said, Behold, I have given you every herb bearing seed, which is upon the face of all the earth, when God says every He means EVERY SEED BEARING HERB !!!

So why is it illegal? We just need to ask Harry Anslinger; but he passed away in 1975, so I wonder if he is in Heaven? According to Wikipedia: Harry Jacob Anslinger (May 20, 1892 – November 14, 1975) held office as the assistant prohibition commissioner in the Bureau of Prohibition, before being appointed as the first commissioner of the U.S. Treasury Department's Federal Bureau of Narcotics (FBN) on August 12, 1930.

Anslinger held office an unprecedented 32 years in his role as commissioner until 1962. He then held office two years as US Representative to the United Nations Narcotics Commission. The responsibilities once held by Anslinger are now largely under the jurisdiction of the U.S. Office of National Drug Control Policy. He died at the age of 83 of heart failure in Altoona, Pennsylvania.

So who would inspire Harry to be so strongly against marijuana. It might have been William Randolph Hearst. That is according to what I have learned visiting Wikipedia. Hearst used the power of his newspaper chain to editorialize for the passage of the Uniform State Narcotic Drug Act after the American Bar Association had approved of it in 1932. Dr. William C. Woodward, legislative counsel of the American Medical Association, suggested the support of the Hearst papers would ensure the passage of the act.[21] Dr. Woodward testified before the House Ways and Means Committee that although "there is no evidence to show whether or not cannabis usage has been increasing" in his opinion "newspaper exploitation of the habit has done more to increase it than anything else.

In 1937 Hearst used his papers to push for the passage of the Marijuana Tax Act of 1937. Hearst was commended by a conference of judges, lawyers and politicians for "pioneering the national fight against dope" for the anti-marijuana editorials and articles in his papers. In later years, however, Hurst's "pioneering" has been widely viewed as mere pandering to the corporate interests of DuPont, as well as protecting his own substantial forest products interests against the industrial use of hemp. Hearst's editorial efforts with respect to the ban on hemp coincide with the court-ordered reorganization of the Hearst corporation's non-publishing assets, mainly mining and forest products, in 1937.

Let's not forget the Box Office Hit, Reefer Madness.

 http://en.wikipedia.org/wiki/Reefer_madness

I wouldn't want to call that film propaganda, but I'll leave my opinion out of this because it's not nice to cuss on this blog, or anywhere. So I will just shut my mouth and finish this dissertation, that Everybody Must Get Stoned with one final thought. Since the corruption involved in the legislation of this Act led to enormous profits for the special interest that promoted it, the law is repugnant to the Constitution and is therefore noll and void.

Oh forget it, I'm going to go smoke a joint and get back to work .on my music.

Thanks You

Colonel Pepper

Rev. Trey Haltom

Falling Figs Music Publishing Company BMI

The Falling Figs Journal Volume 1 Number 1

WRITTEN BY

REV. TREY HALTOM, HIGH PRIEST

THE ORDER OF MELCHIZEDEK AND

FIRST CHURCH OF GOD THE FATHER

808 EAST LAWRENCE LANE STE. # 205

PHOENIX, ARIZONA 85020

FALLING FIGS MUSIC PUBLISHING COMPANY, BMI

A PRESENTATION OF FALLING FIGS PRESS

KATHY DOMINGUEZ, PRESIDENT

fallingfigs@gmail.com

madhavendrapuri@outlook.com

HENRY P. ANSLINGER

HENRY P. ANSLINGER IS RESPONSIBLE FOR ADDING MARIJUANA TO THE TAX ACT OF 1937. THIS MADE IT ILLEGAL TO POSSES, SELL, OR GROW EITHER CANNABIS OR HEMP. THIS WAS DONE AT THE REQUEST OF NEWSPAPER BARON RANDOLPH HURST WHO MADE BILLIONS OF DOLLARS AS A RESULT OF THIS LAW. THE TWO HURST CASTLES IN NORTHERN CALIFORNIA ARE A MONUMENT TO HIS CORRUPTION THAT IS REPUGNANT TO CONSTITUTION AND THEREFORE ACCORDING TO THE LAWS OF THIS NATION ARE NULL AND VOID BY REASON OF THE POLITICAL CORRUPTION AND MANIPULATION OF CONGRESS BY CASH

Mysteries Revealed

What is the secret we do want to know
Said a bunch of fine folk an evening ago
What have we to learn we don't already know
I said take it from me you've a long way to go

Like what are the Mysteries to soon be revealed
Could they be the plagues in the vials that are sealed
Or are they the beasts that arise in the field
I said all of these things should the Mysteries yield

From whence come this answer they asked me pray tell
What manner of wisdom is hidden so well
Is it hid in the word between Heaven and Hell
They're right here on Earth I said in a yell

And their mouths opened wide like the shock in their eyes
This vocal response took them all by surprise
What could this fool know and what makes him so wise
I said I discern between God's truth and lies

And what are the Mysteries to soon be revealed
Could they be the plagues in the vials that are sealed
Or are they the beasts that arise in the field
I said all of these things should the Mysteries yield

But you're just a homeboy a local grown fool
Said a gnarly old boy with a burp and a drool
Then all of them mocked me they thought that was cool
And of coarse I just kicked back I do as a rule

And they thought that a fool ought to be sort of cool
Instead of a dope said this dribbling ghoul
And he uttered and wondered my God what a fool
And I laughed my head off and smoked me a Kool

Yeah and what are the Mysteries to soon be revealed
Could they be the plagues in the vials that are sealed
Or are they the beasts that arise in the field
I said all of these things should the Mysteries yield

(guitar solo)

repeat chorus one time.

Colonel Pepper's Last Stand

1. **Sailor's Destiny**

2. **Foggy Haze of Misty Moods**

3. **I'm Just a Jukebox**

4. **Pie in the Sky**

5. **Southern Justice**

6. **Rode Away**

7. **Wild Man Blues**

8. **Time's Done Changed**

9. **Genie**

10. **My Last Goodbye**

The Songs of God ~ The New Psalms

1. **Foolishness of God**
2. **Damadora**
3. **Ballad of Jesus Christ**
4. **Teachers**
5. **Psalms 64**
6. **Psalms 42**
7. **The Secret Place**
8. **Mysteries Revealed**
9. **Angel Wings**
10. **Fallen Angel**

Colonel Pepper's Last Stand
Sailor's Destiny

Sailing in on the heals of an Angel
Spread His Wings across the sea
On a voyage over oceans and ages
Wondering what's my destiny

    And I'm wondering what's my destiny
    Wondering what's my destiny
    Wondering what's my destiny, Oh Lord

Ship ahoy sailing over the water
Takes my mind from memories
from the bow see the land lovers yonder
Wondering what's my destiny

    And I'm wondering what's my destiny
    Wondering what's my destiny
    Wondering what's my destiny, Oh Lord

I can't recall the days I was not a sailor
It's more than likely I was born out to sea
And when I die send what's left of me starboard
Send my spirit to my Mother the Sea

    And I'm wondering what's my destiny
    Wondering what's my destiny
    Wondering what's my destiny, Oh Lord

Moon and the stars guide me over the water
Four winds blow set my spirit free
Spend my days in the crows nest a watching
Wondering what's my destiny, Oh Lord

    And I'm wondering what's my destiny
    Wondering what's my destiny
    Wondering what's my destiny, Oh Lord

Colonel Pepper's Last Stand
Foggy Haze of Misty Moods

I sit alone when it's cold at night

I sit and think as I try to write

The finest thoughts to bring to you delight

While in my mind you're warming up my lonely night

I take a smoke and light a cigarettes

I take some time and rest my back a bit

And wonder if you even like me yet

Or is this this something I should just forget

    What what have you done to me

    Is this a fantasy or something that I see

    That's only deep inside of me

In my quiet hours of solitude

I wonder what your future plans include

Then your image in my mind eludes

Into the Foggy Haze of Misty Moods

    What what have you done to me

    Is this a fantasy or something that I see

    That's nothing more than make believe

I see us walking by the ocean side

I hear the roaring tide with you by my side

And then we stay there in the moon light

Till the sunrise when this dream subsides

Under the Foggy Haze of Misty Moods

We'll lie forever in the Foggy Haze of Misty Moods

Colonel Pepper's Last Stand
I'm Just a Jukebox

I'm just a Jukebox Put another quarter in the slot

Buy another beer and hear the words to the song you play a lot

This song is nearly worn out but it

Still want's any money that you've got

I'm Just a Jukebox baby put another quarter in the slot

I'm just a jukebox take one more selection if you please

Stay a little longer and set your mind at ease

You can hear the music playing sing along to any song that you request

I'm just a jukebox making music is the thing I do the best

    You see my lady is the barmaid

    And she really turns me on

    When she comes to touch my buttons

    I know my lady wants to boogie all night long

I'm just a Jukebox Put another quarter in the slot

And I'll play for you my music till I've

Taken every quarter that you've got

I'm Just a Jukebox baby put another quarter in the slot

If you want to play my music you will have to pay the fee

I'm just a jukebox I'm your friend but I can never play for free

    You see my lady is the barmaid

    And she really turns me on

    When she comes to touch my buttons

    I know my lady wants to boogie all night long

Colonel Pepper's Last Stand
Pie in the Sky

Life is a short one We understand why
We ain't got no time to be sod or to cry
Be joyful instead and keep on believing
It beats being sad and leaving us grieving
    This is the lesson that needs to be learned
    We reap our rewards and get what we've earned
    But sooner or later we all have to part
    But it's better to leave with an unbroken heart

Give us fair warning to make our amends
To hug all our children and family and friends
Believing the truth we'll be together again
And keep your head high and stick out your chin
    This is the lesson that needs to be learned
    We reap our rewards and get what we've earned
    But sooner or later we all have to part
    But it's better to leave with an unbroken heart

Life is for living so don't live a lie
We always just come back the moment we die
And we all get a piece of the Pie in the Sky
We have it or eat it if we live or we die
    This is the lesson that needs to be learned
    We reap our rewards and get what we've earned
    But sooner or later we all have to part
    But it's better to leave with an unbroken heart

Colonel Pepper's Last Stand
Southern Justice

Well they too away the rambler and they took away his Nash
They said he was a gambler they were looking for his stash
Well they said he was a doper and they put him in a cell
Going to dry out that old boozer in the tank where he is held

And we don't allow no addicts hanging around this town of our-n
We gonna run them out of here with some tar and feathers on
But first we're going to work bloody bohind to the ground
Cut them long and shabby hairs and make them short bald and round

And they took him to his honor and they got him ninety days
And they said he was a wanderer so they made that ten more days
Then they said he was a Yankee so they threw the key away
Oh the blab-by Yankee hippie finally found a place to stay

And we don't allow no addicts hanging around this town of our-n
We gonna run them out of here with some tar and feathers on
But first we're going to work bloody bohind to the ground
Cut them long and shabby hairs and make them short bald and round

Fifteen years on bread and water with some beans some times for lunch
Getting old and gray an honery and his back began to hunch
Oh he'd finally done his time and they punished him enough
He'd do another crime the punishment's to much

And we don't allow no addicts hanging around this town of our-n
We gonna run them out of here with some tar and feathers on
But first we're going to work bloody bohind to the ground
Cut them long and shabby hairs and make them short bald and round

Colonel Pepper's Last Stand
Southern Justice

Southern Justice Southern Justice Southern Justice
Southern Justice What a way to go

And they cut him loose on Sunday on a bus that's no where bound
And they gave him fifty dollars and said never come back around
Then he bought himself a new suit that the tailor painted black
And he bet them fifty dollars he was never coming back

And we don't allow no addicts hanging around this town of our-n
We gonna run them out of here with some tar and feathers on
But first we're going to work bloody bond to the ground
Cut them long and shabby hairs and make them short bald and round

Now the moral of that story is. when he bet them fifty dollars hew was never coming back II they said that constitutes gambling, so he was guilty of not being reformed, and was sentenced to fifty years as a repeat offender.
Do you believe that?
I never heard such a thing

Colonel Pepper

Colonel Pepper's Last Stand
Rode Away

Forlorn or forsaken for some sort of reason
I slipped on my saddle and I just rode away
Rode away from the lady the past stayed behind me
And rode like a blind fool away in the dusk
    And I ride in the evening
    My shadow behind me
    I look for my future
    And I hope it will find me

Be better off staying away from the lady
Who's story is laced with no truth to be found
Be better off living with no one beside me
Just wandering aimless I don't care where I'm bound
    And I ride in the evening
    My shadow behind me
    I look for my future
    And I hope it will find me

A rungy old grungy old son of a gun
With my hat and a beard and alone on the run
I'd be riding to somewhere not sure where I'm going
Whenever I find it I will know I am there
    And I ride in the evening
    My shadow behind me
    I look for my future
    And I hope it will find me

Colonel Pepper's Last Stand
Wild Man Blues

Whoa running around just like a Wild Man

Here we go again

On the path we all began

Lilliputians on a primrose road

Silly cute ones are a heavy load

No back packs no back tracks

Were heading for heaven so don't look back

Drop off your burdens hang up the yoke

And don't laugh at Jesus If you can't take a joke

    Run around like a wild man

    Run around like a wild wild man

    Run around like a wild man

Now watch out for low life riders on the ground

And high flying sissies winging it around

Find one that's sailing solo and bring that mother down

Kick him in the eyeballs turn his head around

The air outside is calm and warm

But in my mind's a raging storm

Stand fast and fight for all that's right

From behind the battle lines through the bloody night

    Run around like a wild man

    Run around like a wild wild man

    Run around like a wild man`

You know I thought I'd seen everything

I thought I sang everything there was to sing

Looked square in the face of the human race

Colonel Pepper's Last Stand
Wild Man Blues

Conquered every foe that I really know

No back packs no back tracks

Headed for heaven so don't look back

Drop off your burdens hang up the yoke

And don't laugh at Jesus If you can't take a joke

    Run around like a wild man

    Run around like a wild wild man

    Run around like a wild man`

Kill off the enemies knock off the foes

Pick om anybody step on their toes

Show them their pitfalls turn them all around

Show the coarse they are headed for

Will never never leave the ground

Kiss the pretty ladies love all the rest

Take them to Heaven give them your best

Watch out for humor it might make you choke

And don't fuck with Satan if you don't like smoke

    Run around like a wild man

    Run around like a wild wild man

    Run around like a wild man`

    Run around like a wild man

    Run around like a wild wild man

    Run around like a wild man`

    Run around like a wild man

This song is dedicated to Sonny Barger,

Founder & President

of the Hell's Angels Motorcycle Club.

Colonel Pepper's Last Stand
My Last Goodbye

Before my days are ever ended
I look toward the sky and cry
For all the days I've spent are wasted
So now I'll sat my Last Goodbye

    Bye Bye Bye Bye

Farewell to those that never knew me
Fir there are stranger things than I
And who's to say what has inspired me
And who can say I did not try

    Bye Bye Bye Bye
    This is my My Last Goodbye
    Bye Bye Bye Bye
    This is my My Last Goodbye

Cause In a world that's filled with sorrow
Yeah it's a world that's filled with pain
Will I still be here tomorrow
Or stand alone and watch the rain

    Bye Bye Bye Bye

For when these Irish eyes are crying
Clouds appear and block the sky
And Heaven stays behind them hiding
Until the tears have left my eyes

    Bye Bye Bye Bye
    This is my My Last Goodbye
    Bye Bye Bye Bye
    This is my My Last Goodbye
    Bye Bye Bye Bye Bye Bye

New Psalms ~ The Songs of God
Foolishness of God

I'd walk in a fiery furnace like a fool inside a flame

And I'd do it for your glory Lord while trusting in your name

Then I'd set my face towards this land and warn them while there is time

Cause the end is just beginning And we all must make our minds

    Because the Foolishness of God Is so much wiser than a man

    That I wonder why I even try They just do not understand `

    Lord it breaks my heart in pieces   Knowing what will come to pass

    And if I try to tell them will they hear my song at last

Surely they are smart enough to mend their wicked ways

Well I believe they would if they only knew They were living numbered days

Well I forgive them for the things they've done They could not find their way

It's the leaders who have deceived them and they led them all astray

    But the Foolishness of God Is so much wiser than a man

    That I wonder why I just don't try To make them understand

    Lord it breaks my heart in pieces   Knowing what will come to pass

    Cause if I try to tell them Lord will they hear my song at last

    Oh Lord will they hear my song at last

The troubles in this world could cause a politicians fall

While the plagues the rest all die from do not sound like aid at all

And the teachers teach them foolishness and that's a scientific fact

That they can not cure the common cold or stop a heart attack

    Because the Foolishness of God Is so much wiser than a man

    That I wonder why I even try They just do not understand

    Lord it breaks my heart in pieces Knowing what will come to pass

    And if I try to tell them will they hear my song at last

    Because the Foolishness of God Is so much wiser than a man

New Psalms ~ The Songs of God
Foolishness of God

Yeah the Foolishness of God Is so much wiser than a man
You know the Foolishness of God   Is so much wiser than a man

And now I know why I just have to try I've got to make them understand
Because it breaks my heart in pieces Knowing what will come to pass
So I sing your glory Lord and I sing your song at last

Cause the Foolishness of God Is so much wiser than a man
You know the Foolishness of God Is so much wiser than a man

The Foolishness of God Is wiser than a man
The Foolishness of God is wiser
The Foolishness of God Is wiser than a man
The Foolishness of God is wiser

New Psalms ~ The Songs of God
Ballad of Jesus Christ

Those that He had chosen had rejected Him the most

In the midst of the commotion Oh they bound the Lord of Host

And then savagely they beat Him and scourged him with a whip

That left His flesh in tatters from the metal on the tip

And they took a tree and shaped it and they made a rugged cross

And then nailed the Lord onto it oh for this would be the cost

The price for my salvation is much more than I can pay

The Lamb from the Foundation was slain and is the way

And the people were so blinded by inequity and sin

That they could not see old Satan in the background with a grin

That living bleak obscenity God's rival from the start

But soon they would all plainly see the broken Sacred Heart

Abba it is finished spoke the Lord in His despair

As the clouds brought on the darkness and the stillness in the air

And Satan and his army must have trembled at this sight

Cause when the Lord departed He took away the light

Forsaken almost broken he has given up the ghost

And then Pilot sent his centuries to guard the Lord of Host

And while the guards were sleeping He arose and walked away

And just as He had promised He would rise on the third day

Ans then Jesus told the brothers they must go and feed the sheep

For a flock without a shepherd is impossible to keep

And Peter had a mission the disciples had an aim

With the Pentecostal fire let the good news be proclaimed

Before the Lord ascended to be seated in His place

By the right hand of the Father who had made the human race

He said the victory is faith and we need not live in fear

For whenever we are gathered we may know that He is near

For whenever we are gathered we may know that He is nere

New Psalms ~ The Songs of God
Teachers

He said Preacher don't be too hard on me this morning

Cause I had a hard night last night and my head is spinning

Well I hope you don't preach too long on sinning

Cause I've got to get home by noon to see who's winning

    Well they heaped unto themselves ooh many teachers

    And they are scratching their itching ears

Now the women want liberation who's going to free them

Cut the bonds that tie them down into the kitchen

Send the children to the state for education

Let them study all them books about evolution

    Well they heaped unto themselves ooh many teachers

    And they're scratching their itching ears

There are signs along the roadside can you see them

Well they are there to tell you all which way to go

And there are signs of the times can you discern them

Well they are there for every one to know

The sheep have leaders their fleece is held by a zipper

Yes and the lies they spread they could not make me sicker

    And they heaped unto themselves ooh many teachers

    And they're scratching their itching ears

And they said Preacher don't talk to us about the demons

On no or spiritual powers we don't believe in

Our god's a good god He will not harm us oh he won't harm us

So if you want to keep your job just don't alarm us

    And they heaped unto themselves ooh many teachers

    And they are scratching their itching ears

    Yeah they heaped unto themselves ooh many teachers

    And they're searching their empty hearts for love

New Psalms ~ The Songs of God
Psalms 64

As I wander through this dry and thirsty land

Where no water falls upon the dusty sand

There I thirst for you and I long for you in my flesh

Early will I seek you in your power

Early will I find you in your glory

Because your love is so much better

Your loving kindness is better than life

 I will praise you and lift up my hands in your name

 I will praise you from my mouth with joyful lips

 Uphold me with your right hand

 Hide me in the shadows of your wings

 And I will rejoice

 Uphold me with your right hand

 Hide me in the shadows of your wings

Oh God you are my God earnestly I seek you

My soul thirsts for you in a dry and weary land

Where there is no water and because your love is better than life

My lips will glorify you I will praise you as long as I live

And in your name I will lift up my hands

 I will praise you and lift up my hands in your name

 I will praise you from my mouth with joyful lips

 Uphold me with your right hand

 Hide me in the shadows of your wings

 And I will rejoice

 Uphold me with your right hand

 Hide me in the shadows of your wings

Lord Lord Lord Lord Jesus

Oh my Lord I will rejoice

Lord Lord Lord Lord Jesus

Uphold me with your right hand

Hide me in the shadows of your wings

New Psalms ~ the Songs of God
Psalms 42

As the heart panteth after the water brooks

So panteth my soul after The of God

My soul thirsts for God for the Living God

When shall I come and appear before God

My tears have been my meat both day and night

While they say unto me continually

Where is thy God thy Living God

When shall I come and appear before God

    Who am I where am I going

    What will I be in the end

    Deep calls unto deep

    Thy ways are gone over me

    Yes the Lord will call His love to me

As the heart panteth after the water brooks

So panteth my soul after The of God

My soul thirsts for God for the Living God

When shall I come and appear before God

    Who are you where are you going

    What will you be in the end

    Why is my soul cast down before me

    Why have you forgotten me oh my God

    Who am I where am I going

    What will I be in the end

    Deep calls unto deep

    And thy ways are gone over me

    Yet the Lord will call His love to me

As the heart panteth after the water brooks

So panteth my soul after The of God

My soul thirsts for God for the Living God

When shall I come and appear before God

New Psalms ~ the Songs of God
Mysteries Revealed

So what is the secret we do want to know
Said a bunch of fine folk an evening ago
What have we to learn we don't already know
I said take it from me you've a long way to go
    Like what are the mysteries to soon be revealed
    Could they be the plagues in the vials that are sealed
    Or are they the beasts that arise in the field
    I said all of these things should the mysteries yield
From whence comes this answer they asked me pray tell
What manner of wisdom is hidden so well
Is it hid in the word between Heaven and Hell
They're right here on Earth I said in a yell
And their mouths opened wide like the shock in their eyes
This vocal response took them all by surprise
What could this fool know and what makes him so wise
I said I discern between God's truth and lies
    And what are the mysteries to soon be revealed
    Could they be the plagues in the vials that are sealed
    Or are they the beasts that arise in the field
    I said all of these things should the mysteries yield
But you're just a homeboy a local grown fool
Said a gnarly old boy with a burp and a drool
Then all of them mocked me they thought that was cool
And of coarse I just kicked back I do as a rule
And they thought that a fool ought to be sort of cool
Instead of a dope said a dribbling ghoul
And he uttered and wondered my God what a fool
And I laughed my head off and smoked me a Kool

New Psalms ~ the Songs of God
Angel's Wings

If you're looking down your nose a me you will never see my wings

But if you'd lend those ears to me I could show you many things

It's not the words to the songs I sing that makes you laugh and cry

It's when we come together and the times we say goodbye

Sometimes I find you're on my mind   Sometimes I find worth saving

It's times like these I'm on my knees   The times I find I'm praying

Sometimes I find you're on my mind   Sometimes I find I'm crying

And it's times like this I's rather miss   It's the times I find so trying

And if you're looking down your nose at me   Well you will never see my wings

If you're looking down your nose a me you will never see my wings

And if you'd lend those ears to me I could show you many things

And if you'd walk a mile with me I'd show you where I've been

Spend some time and you would smile with me and we'll both remember when

Sometimes I find you're on my mind   Sometimes I find worth saving

And it's times like these I'm on my knees   The times I find I'm praying

Sometimes I find you're on my mind   Sometimes I find I'm crying

And it's times like this I'd rather miss   The times I find so trying

And if you're looking down your nose at me   You will never see my wings

New Psalms ~ the Songs of God
Fallen Angel

And God saw that the wickedness of man was great in the Earth

And then every imagination of the thoughts of his heart was only evil continually

But Noah found grace in the eyes of the Lord

The Sons of God came down from Heaven bore children with the daughters of men

They crossed over boundaries they never should have

Creating giants called the Nephilim They fell to Earth from wars lost in Heaven

And their flesh is their prison now They carried demons

but in their heart of hearts they know

> *Sometimes I feel like a Fallen Angel Sometimes I feel like I've died*
>
> *Sometimes I feel like a Fallen Angel All because of my pride*

Enoch was born the seventh from Adam Great Grandfather to Noah of the Ark

He told the story about the fall of the rebel Angels and mans great trek into the dark

The ungodly race of Cain was finding carnal affection

Seeds they called the children of men and now they've fallen

> *Sometimes I feel like a Fallen Angel Sometimes I feel like I've died*
>
> *Sometimes I feel like a Fallen Angel I need some peace at any cost*

Fallen Angel the samples that I've showed is not the life that I would lead

Fallen Angel if I's only comprehend the consequences of my deeds

They taught the hidden craft of boring masses and steal eternal secrets from above

Whats loosed in Heaven will be loosed on Earth

> *Sometimes I feel like a Fallen Angel Sometimes I feel like I've died*
>
> *Sometimes I feel like a Fallen Angel All because of my pride*

And this is the condemnation Fallen Angel That light has come into the world

And men loved darkness rather than light Fallen Angel because their deeds were evil

Lord have mercy on this Fallen Angel Lord have mercy on us all

Lord have mercy on this Fallen Angel Lord have mercy on us all

God have mercy on this Fallen Angel God have mercy on us all

Now unto Him that is able to keep you from falling

And to present you flawless into the presence of His glory

With exceeding joy to the only wise God our Savior

Be glory and majesty dominion and power both now and forever Amen

Made in the USA
Monee, IL
21 March 2024